Please renew/return this item by the last date shown.

So that your telephone call is charged at local rate,
please call the numbers as set out below:

	From Area codes 01923 or 020:	From the rest of Herts:
Renewals:	01923 471373	01438 737373
Enquiries:	01923 471333	01438 737333
Textphone:	01923 471599	01438 737599

L32   www.hertsdirect.org/librarycatalogue

THE STORY OF THE CORONATION

THE STORY
OF THE
CORONATION

by

RANDOLPH S. CHURCHILL

DEREK VERSCHOYLE
13 PARK PLACE, ST JAMES'S, LONDON S.W.1

First published in 1953 by
Derek Verschoyle Limited
Thirteen Park Place St James's
London SW1

MADE AND PRINTED IN GREAT BRITAIN
AT THE CHAPEL RIVER PRESS, ANDOVER, HANTS

CONTENTS

ILLUSTRATIONS

FOREWORD

BY
SIR GEORGE BELLEW
GARTER KING OF ARMS

Too many people look upon the Coronation as a whole as simply a magnificent spectacle and an occasion for rejoicing. This indeed it is, but it is also a very significant event in our history.

At this time, when the day on which it will take place is rapidly approaching, surely it is both right and rewarding to learn as much as possible about it. The ceremony within the Abbey is the essence of the Coronation and it is unfortunately the part of it which is the least understood. This book provides a means of gaining a greater knowledge of its true significance and also of its historical background.

Not everyone will agree with all the judgments and opinions expressed by Mr Randolph Churchill. His approach to some aspects of his subject is controversial, but this may be found refreshing. In any event one cannot but respect the application and research which the author has evidently devoted to his complicated task.

20 February 1953

PART I

CHAPTER 1

HER MAJESTY QUEEN ELIZABETH II

> The Monarchy is to-day regarded by the people of this island and of the Commonwealth and Empire as the magnet of loyalty, the emblem of union, the symbol of continuity and the embodiment of national, as distinct from class or party, feeling.

The varied duties of a constitutional monarchy have never been defined so clearly and so compendiously as in these words of Sir Harold Nicolson in his admirable and fascinating biography of King George V, published last year. How well equipped is Queen Elizabeth II to discharge this truly awe-inspiring catalogue of functions?

It is part of the cant of the Century of the Common Man and the Common Woman to assert that sovereigns who ascend the throne, without in their youth having expected to do so, have great advantages over those who were predestined to rule from birth. The case of his late Majesty, King George VI, is often cited in this connection. George VI was a much beloved and highly successful constitutional king but there seems very little evidence to support the theory that he would have been a less good king if he had been the elder, instead of the younger brother of King Edward VIII.

Be that as it may, Queen Elizabeth II always stood very close in succession to the throne. When she was born in 1926, her uncle, who was then Prince of Wales, was thirty-two years old and unmarried. Thus from her birth there was always a likelihood that she would one day succeed to the throne. She was only ten years old when her uncle abdicated and it became a virtual certainty that she would one day be Queen. The art, for such it is, of being a constitutional sovereign is not fundamentally one that can be learnt at school or in text books; though these may help. Heredity may play a part but environment is usually the decisive factor. Statecraft, no less than banking, baking, brewing or shop-keeping, has often thrived as a family business, because the principles upon which it is practised are most easily and painlessly assimilated at an early age. A boy who has helped his father in his shop or business will often find that he has acquired, through the environment of his home life, a natural bent for such work. And a princess who has spent her later childhood in a royal palace, knowing that she will one day inherit her father's kingly problems and responsibilities is more likely, other things being equal, to find herself adequate to the role than someone who never had any such expectation, training or environment.

It is therefore foolish to nourish the prosaic fallacy that the Queen had just the same sort of upbringing and education as the daughters of some thousands of her father's more prosperous subjects. Of course she had to be taught to read and write and do her sums; and there are not a great variety of methods by which these rudimentary lessons may be taught. Of course in the nursery and the schoolroom she was subjected to discipline and she associated on level terms with other girls of her own age. But nothing could conceal, or ought to have concealed from her the unique destiny that lay ahead and which, through the untimely death of her father, was to confront her at the age of twenty-five.

*   *   *

One can never know what is the real education of a prince or princess. Royalties live in a world of their own and are never quite themselves when other people are present; but it is evident that the most valuable part of the Queen's education was that she grew to womanhood in a happy family, cared for and guided by sensible parents who realised the tremendous task which would one day be hers and who did all in their power to see that she grew up to be a good and happy human being. Her father, her grandfather King George V and her great-grandfather King Edward VII all grew up in tremendous awe of their parents, and none of them could be said to have had a happy childhood. The late King adored his daughters and used to allow them to tease and chaff him to their hearts content.

Publicists who have sought to suggest that immense pains and effort were lavished upon her education and that the Queen is almost a latter-day Lady Jane Grey are very wide of the mark. In fact, Queen Elizabeth the Queen Mother has rather old-fashioned views on how girls should be brought up. She did not believe in stuffing them full of book learning. She never aimed at more than bringing her daughters up to be nicely behaved young ladies. She had no intellectual ambitions for them.

The nursery governess, Miss Crawford, who went to the Palace when the Queen was seven was not a woman of any great erudition; but the two Princesses were so happy under her light tutelage that she remained in charge of the Queen's education until she was seventeen, her efforts being supplemented by the Vicomtesse de Bellaigue who for some years gave the Princesses a grounding in French. In addition, for a short time during the war, the Queen received tuition in constitutional history from the late Sir Henry Marten, then Vice-Provost of Eton.

Strangely enough, their mother never encouraged either of the Princesses to play golf or tennis, though the late King played the latter game well enough to enter several times at Wimbledon, and was also a good golfer. On the other hand, the Queen has a deep love of country pursuits. She is never happier than when walking with her dogs. She is a competent and enthusiastic angler and an excellent rifle shot. Her favourite pastime is stalking and she has killed many stags in the deer forests around Balmoral. She is also fond of riding and has a good seat on a horse. In recent years she has acquired a serious interest in racing and has a genuine knowledge of it. Her principal drawing-room accomplishment is playing the piano, although she has not as great a natural aptitude for this as has Princess Margaret. Like most people under thirty the Queen has never savoured the delights of the Bridge table. In common with so many of her generation she has fallen a victim of that great social evil, Canasta. She is, however, far less addicted to this sad amusement than either her sister or her mother.

The greatest qualities which the Queen brings to the service of her people are those of character. She feels a genuine sense of dedication to her task and has plenty of determination. All who know her well praise her powers of judgement and decision. Her critical faculties are well developed. Everybody who works with the Queen or knows her well suspects a considerable strength of will, perhaps even a streak of obstinacy, under her radiant manner. She has strong opinions of her own on many topics. If her initiative is in many ways less marked than her powers of criticism, this must be accounted a blessing in a constitutional monarch. Having grown up in her father's house she has an instinctive understanding alike of the potentialities and the limitations of her position; and arduous though her duties will be, her abundant common sense and natural sense of humour should enable her to discharge them and still lead the full and happy family life which all her subjects pray may long be hers.

Though a modern constitutional Queen may accumulate and exercise much influence, she can have little direct political power. With one exception, even the Royal Prerogative can only be used in accordance with ministerial advice. The exception is in the choice of a Prime Minister, and even this opportunity has only arisen four times in the last sixty years. Almost always when a Prime Minister dies or resigns, the choice of a new Prime Minister admits of no dispute, since there is usually only one man who can command a majority in the House of Commons. However, when Mr Gladstone resigned in 1894 and again when Mr Bonar Law resigned in 1923 there were two contestants for the succession to the leadership of the dominant party.

In the first case Queen Victoria preferred Lord Rosebery to Sir William Harcourt; in the second King George V set aside the claims of Lord Curzon in favour of the obscure Mr Baldwin. In 1929, when Mr. Baldwin resigned following his electoral defeat, the King sent for Mr Ramsay MacDonald without consulting Mr Baldwin. But on this occasion any other choice would have been virtually impossible. The fourth occasion was in 1931 when it was the King's personal decision to persuade Mr Ramsay MacDonald to head the National Government in preference to any of the other arrangements that were open.

An outgoing Prime Minister has no right to volunteer advice to the sovereign as to the choice of his successor. In normal cases, however, the sovereign would consult him. Mr Bonar Law, who was dying of cancer, was too ill to be consulted in 1923. Queen Victoria chose not to consult Mr Gladstone in 1895. If she had done so Mr Gladstone would have recommended Lord Spencer.

*   *   *

When Charles II was told of the epitaph which Lord Rochester had written for him:

> Here lies our sovereign lord the King
> Whose promise none relies on;
> He never said a foolish thing
> Nor ever did a wise one,

he is supposed to have commented: 'That is very true; for my words are my own and my actions are my ministers'.' Thus, even under the later Stuarts, the doctrine that the sovereign must act upon the advice of ministers was already germinating in men's minds.

14

The theory that the King can do no wrong was originally an expression of the autocratic will of the Tudors and the Stuarts. It is still sound constitutional theory, but over the last two hundred years it has increasingly been interpreted to mean that if the Government is at fault it is the ministers, not the sovereign, who are to blame, since a constitutional sovereign can only act on the advice of ministers.

Over the last hundred years, however, the same doctrine has gained such total acceptance that paradoxically the reverse is now true. Since the sovereign can only act on the advice of ministers, it is unnecessary, except in a purely formal sense, that advice should be tendered. It has become a figure of speech to talk of 'giving advice' to a constitutional sovereign; on the other hand the sovereign frequently gives advice to ministers which is often, though by no means always, accepted. To put it another way; three hundred years ago ministers advised, the sovereign decided. To-day the cycle has come full circle; ministers decide, the sovereign advises.

In the matter of appointments where the Queen is likely to have a view of her own, her informal approval is invariably sought before advice is tendered. So far as general policy is concerned, the Prime Minister has a weekly audience with the Queen so that he may give an account of the Government's intentions and make sure that the Sovereign has no objections to the proposals which the Government intends to put forward in the Sovereign's name.

The longer a sovereign has sat upon the throne, the more experienced he or she will be and Sir Harold Nicolson has shown how frequently and sagaciously King George V advised his ministers and how often they accepted what he counselled. The sovereign is above the strife of party politics and is likely to have a far more deeply ingrained instinct for the traditions and interests of the nation than most politicians. The triple role of a modern constitutional sovereign, which Bagheot so happily described as 'to advise, to encourage and to warn', will no doubt be progressively discharged by the Queen as she becomes increasingly experienced in the arts of government.

CHAPTER 2

THE HISTORY AND SIGNIFICANCE OF
THE CORONATION

'The coronation ceremonies of England constitute one of the most striking examples of conservatism. This is due no doubt to the character of the service; its essentials cannot be changed, and it is also due to the fact that it is only rarely performed. It is, and always has been, a service consecrating the new King with certain fixed rites: unction and the delivery of royal ornaments. In return for the reception of these gifts the King has always bound himself by certain promises. Such is the naked outline of the service.' So wrote Mr Wickham Legg in 1901 in his scholarly work *English Coronation Records*.

In the early history of England the actual crowning ceremony was not necessarily thought to be the most important part of the coronation. By some it was considered only incidental to the King's election and anointing. In recent centuries the doctrine of 'The King is dead, long live the King' has become formally established. Since the Whig Revolution of 1688 brought Dutch William to the throne, the Crown must constitutionally be deemed to be in the gift of Parliament. Yet the heir to the throne automatically becomes the Sovereign on the death of his predecessor. If Parliament wished to make other arrangements it would, presumably, do so well in advance. Election has ceased, but a potential power of veto certainly remains. Since the thirteenth century the Crown of England has been hereditary, but this principle has long been subject to the ultimate sanction of Parliament.

Edward VI, son of Henry VIII and Lady Jane Seymour, who succeeded his father at the age of ten was, strangely enough, the first English King who claimed the throne without election. Three days after the death of his father he declared with his own signature and that of his Council that he had come to the throne. 'Le Roi est mort! Vive le Roi!'

In Saxon and Norman times Kings were elected; and it was only after they had been chosen by the Nobles that they went in procession to Westminster Abbey so that the Prince or Noble who had

RD   REX

been elected might be anointed and crowned. In practice the choice usually lay between a small number of possible heirs. In the thirteenth century primogeniture became established.

In Norman times, and still more during the troubled days of the Wars of the Roses in the fifteenth century, the first step taken by the probable candidate for the throne was to instal himself in the Tower of London. Only there did he feel secure while his friends and adherents organised his election and coronation; and it is significant that one of the first steps taken in those days was for the man who thought he had a claim to the throne to appoint an Earl Marshal to take over Westminster Abbey and prepare it for the coronation. The ancestor of the present Duke of Norfolk was the Commander-in-Chief of the Army in 1483. He was selected by Richard III to organise his coronation. Everything went off well, but two years later both the King and his Earl Marshal were defeated and killed at the Battle of Bosworth and the Tudors came to power.

From 1054 the Saxon kings began to reside in Westminster. But from the twelfth century onwards when the Tower of London had been completed, the first stage of a coronation was a procession the day before from the Tower to Westminster Hall. This procession was abandoned at the Coronation of James II. The King-to-be spent the night in the Palace of Westminster (in later years in the Speaker's House). Early on Coronation morning he processed into Westminster Hall where, under a Cloth of Estate, he was elected by acclamation and enthroned by the Peers. It was only after this had been done that the Royal procession moved on to Westminster Abbey for the anointing and crowning.

Until the accession of Edward I in 1272, the kings of England dated their reigns not from the death of their predecessors, but from the date of their coronations. Prior to the establishment of the now-vanished ceremony in Westminster Hall, a form of election was gone through in the Abbey.

At the coronation of King John in the year 1199 Archbishop Walter, mistrusting the character of John, insisted on an election in order to lessen his responsibility in crowning such a man. Subsequent events which culminated at Runnymede in 1215 when the Barons forced King John to seal Magna Carta confirmed the Archbishop's prescience. Even in modern times, at the outset of the coronation service, the people 'recognize' and acclaim the Sovereign. Thus a vestigial relic of election is still preserved.

King Edward the Confessor

The last English king whose coronation included the ceremony in Westminster Hall and the procession on foot to the Abbey, followed by a banquet in Westminster Hall, was George IV. His coronation was, perhaps, the most magnificent pageant ever staged. He spent so much money on it that his brother William IV who succeeded him suggested to his Prime Minister, Earl Grey, that perhaps he might dispense with a coronation altogether. The Prime Minister could not accept this, but it was done very much 'on the cheap' and became known as the 'half-crowning'.

Last year, when preparations for the coronation of Queen Elizabeth II were being discussed, a proposal was put forward in Mr Dermot Morrah's *The Round Table* that the ancient ceremonies of election and enthroning in Westminster Hall should be revived. Apart from reviving a noble ceremony, it was felt that if the Peers, who now number more than 850, were to have this splendid show to themselves, there might be fewer hard feelings among them if their numbers in the Abbey were curtailed so as to provide more room for other people. Although the proposal was made nine months before the Coronation, officialdom took the view that the suggestion came too late. As Garter King of Arms, Sir George Bellew, once sagaciously observed, 'the time for making suggestions for alterations in the ceremony is after a coronation and not before it'.

Though these time-honoured ceremonies lapsed with George IV, his concept of pageantry survived the frugal instincts of William IV and there are those who regret that what was once a serious political and religious ceremony now tends often to be regarded as a public spectacle, which some would like to degrade still further into a three-ring circus. The Church, the Royal Family and those who would like to feel that England was still a Christian country, in more than name, naturally wish that the sacred and sacramental aspects of the coronation which it has always had should still be present in the public mind. The importance of these spiritual aspects will be discussed in the next chapter.

From the Middle Ages onward many European dynasties accepted the Salic Law by which daughters were excluded from the succession. In England, heirs of the body, including daughters, have the right to succeed in accordance with the degree of their relationship to the Sovereign. Since, in the past, English princesses have tended to marry foreigners, Scottish, Dutch, Hanoverians and Coburgs have all succeeded to the throne. Increasing nationalism, combined with the decay or disappearance of European royal houses, has led to a change in public sentiment which would now be opposed to the importation of any further foreign dynasty.

It is significant in this connection that prior to the announcement of his engagement to Princess Elizabeth, Prince Philip of Greece, as he then was, became a British subject and abandoned his foreign title.

Modern constitutional doctrine about the Monarchy may be briefly summarised as follows: the Queen came to the throne at the moment of her father's death; but her accession required consecration and confirmation by the ceremonies of anointing and coronation. Though the Queen's accession was automatic, she did not announce it herself. This was done by the Accession Council, which at one time used to elect the Sovereign. Confirmation of the Queen's accession by the people is still inherent in the question which the Archbishop puts to the congregation at the beginning of the coronation service. But the dynastic principle has triumphed and is enshrined in the very heart of the theory of a modern constitutional monarchy, as it is, if we search our hearts, in ourselves.

CHAPTER 3

THE SPIRITUAL AND POLITICAL ASPECTS

The earliest records of the ceremony of crowning Kings, whether in France, Germany or England, show that it has always been considered as an act of a sacramental character. A sacrament has been best defined 'as the outward and visible sign of an inward and spiritual grace'. Throughout history Christian Kings, whether they gained the throne by election, heredity or force, have always deemed it expedient to have their assumption of power sanctified by the church.

In the middle-ages great disputes raged as to how far the nature of a King was transformed by the ceremony of anointing which is the central and vital act in the whole service. Kings vied with each other to obtain from the Pope the right to be anointed with the chrism which is used in the anointing of Bishops, instead of merely with the simple oil which is available to catechumens.

These controversies have long grown stale but the ceremonies which survive indicate that the anointing was intended to give to the earthly ruler some of the sanctity of a priest. And the coronation oath is not only a compact which the Sovereign enters into with his people to respect the laws and customs of the land, but also a solemn acceptance of the fact that the role of ruler can only be rightly discharged under divine sanction and providence.

Dr A. P. Purey-Cust, the late Dean of York, writing in 1911 put the point in this way 'the church is the witness to the contract between the rulers and their subjects – in other words, religion is a safeguard on the one hand for the freedom of the people, and on the other for the authority of the chief magistrate'.

The most authoritative work on the history and theory of the English coronation service was written by a German, Percy Ernst Schramm, Professor of History in the University of Gottenburg. Professor Schramm, who writes with unchallengeable scholarship and pith, has made a life-time study of the history of coronations. In 1937, just prior to the coronation of King George VI, he published 'A History of the English Coronation.' This book has now become the standard work on the subject.

Schramm's opening paragraph epitomises the whole concept of monarchy:

'Le Roi est mort, vive le Roi!' The doctrine underlying this famous proclamation by the French herald is that the successor to the throne enters upon his office at the moment of his predecessor's death, and it has been summed up in the epigram that the King never dies. The King is always there; but from time to time a herald proclaims that his name has been changed.

But Schramm almost immediately adds the rider

if the successor is to become King in the fullest sense, he must first be inaugurated into the government by legal and ecclesiastical rites.

The idea of an hereditary monarchy has developed through the ages and its origins go back beyond the memory of man. But certainly in the Christian era, except for various periods of absolutism and tyranny, the concept of the Sovereign accepting the laws of God and the laws of man as a condition precedent to receiving the acceptance and the loyalty of his people has increasingly prevailed.

During the middle-ages the church, which rivalled the monarchy in wealth, authority and power, exerted herself to impose conditions upon Kings which would safeguard not only the church's spiritual authority but her material possessions. English Kings like John found themselves as much frustrated from their goal of absolutism by Popes and Cardinals as they did by the barons at Runnymede. Kings were therefore glad to make concessions to the church in return for the privilege of being anointed, for this ceremony imparted to them the mystical and sacrosanct aura which usually shrouded the priesthood from violence.[1]

Thus the spiritual aspect of anointing which goes back to the Kings in the Old Testament, was enhanced by a practical value. A King who could not persuade a Bishop to anoint and crown him was a King in name only and his reign was subject to early abridgement. It is a profitless task to try to re-write Schramm: – 'What was the political significance of this ecclesiastical ceremony?' he asks. 'The holy oil separated the King from his subjects, made him like the priest, conjoined him with other kings, and gave him precedence over those who did not enjoy the right.'

In the middle-ages there were only, apart from the Holy Roman Emperor, four Christian Kings who enjoyed the privilege of being anointed; they were the Kings of England, France, Jerusalem and

[1] Mr Wickham Legg in his *Coronation Records* points out that what aggravated the crime of the murderers of Thomas à Becket was 'the injury they inflicted on the crown of his head which had received unction with the chrism'.

Sicily. Later this privilege was also accorded to the King of Scotland. There were, however, twenty-two Christian Kings who were neither anointed nor crowned. Only the Kings of England and of France had the special right of being anointed with the holy oil or chrism, a word derived from the Greek $X\rho\iota\sigma\mu\alpha$.[1]

From time immemorial in the Western Church on Maundy Thursday three different oils have been blessed by the Bishop to be used in the baptisms on the night before Easter: – the oil of the sick, the oil of the catechumens (these were of ordinary olive oil) and the cream which is a mixture of olive oil and balm. The cream is used only in the most sacred ceremonies of the church: in administering confirmations, in the ordination of priests and in the consecration of Bishops. It was thus held to be a special vehicle for the communication of the Holy Ghost.

In his 'The Sacring of the English Kings' Wickham Legg asserts

> in fact, there are traces of a popular opinion, not however allowed by authority, that as the second person of the Holy Trinity is present in the eucharist, so the third person of the Holy Trinity resided in the cream.

The chrism has been used in the crowning of English Kings at least since the coronation of Edward II in 1307. In the order for his coronation it was appointed that the sign of the Cross on the King's head should be made with cream. For the other places which were anointed, only the oil of catechumens was used. In the fourteenth century it was done in this order: first the hands, then the breast and between the shoulders, then the shoulders and the elbows. Finally the sign of the Cross was twice made on the King's head and it was only these last two crosses which were made with the chrism. The Kings of France were anointed in the same places but in the reverse order, starting on the head and ending on the hands. In France a small drop was added to the holy cream from the Ampulla which was believed, by a miracle, to have been brought down from heaven at the time of the baptism of Clovis. It is alleged that the French Ampulla was publicly destroyed in Rheims during the French Revolution.

The sanctity which was supposed to attach to the person of a King who had the blessing of the church is well illustrated by Shakespeare when he makes Richard II at the nadir of his fortunes assert:

[1] $X\rho\iota\sigma\tau\delta s$, from which the word Christ is derived, means the 'Anointed'.

Not all the water in the rough rude sea
Can wash the balm from an anointed king;
The breath of worldly men cannot depose
The deputy elected by the Lord.
For every man that Bolingbroke hath press'd
To lift shrewd steel against our golden crown,
God for his Richard hath in heavenly pay
A glorious angel; then, if angels fight,
Weak men must fall, for heaven still guards the right.

A Saxon Abbot, Aelfric, postulated this claim nearly a thousand years ago when he said 'After he has been hallowed to King, he has power over the people, and they cannot shake his yoke from off their shoulders.' The church plainly drove a hard bargain with the King and the King was inclined to exploit his side of the bargain to the maximum.

The idea that the King after being anointed had become a mystical being early led to the idea that he had miraculous powers of healing. Being touched for the King's Evil was regarded for many hundreds of years as a cure for scrofula; and this power, when ratified by anointing, was believed to be hereditary.[1] Malcolm returning from England is represented in Macbeth as saying of Edward the Confessor:

... How he solicits heaven,
Himself best knows: but strangely-visited people,
All swoln and ulcerous, pitiful to the eye,
The mere despair of surgery, he cures;
Hanging a golden stamp about their necks,
Put on with holy prayers: and 'tis spoken,
To the succeeding royalty he leaves
The healing benediction. With this strange virtue,
He hath a heavenly gift of prophecy;
And sundry blessings hang about his throne,
That speak him full of grace.

Just as the King had practical need of the benediction of the church so the church had need of him to safeguard their wide and growing properties. Thus there was often fierce competition among the Archbishops and Bishops as to who should have the prescriptive right of placing the crown on the Sovereign's head.

In the tenth and eleventh centuries there was much altercation between the sees of Canterbury and York as to the right of crowning the King. From the twelfth century onwards the right of

[1] Another view is that the gift arose out of St. Edward's personal sanctity and that it was conveyed to his successors through their being consecrated with his relics.

Canterbury was so firmly established that at the coronation of Henry III in 1216 Stephen Langton Archbishop of Canterbury who was abroad was deputised for, not by the Archbishop of York, but by the Bishop of Winchester as Suffragan of Canterbury. From this time forward there has been no further dispute in the matter.[1]

Out of the dynastic and religious quarrels in the middle-ages has emerged a monarchy buttressed by tradition, fortified by law and hallowed and sanctified by God's blessing, communicated by the church. In the Communion Service the Sovereign accepts the Sceptre with the Dove as the visible reminder of the fact that in the Communion Service the Sovereign receives the sevenfold Gift of the Holy Ghost.

[1] It is easy to see the importance of confining the right to Canterbury. If York were to have the right of crowning a King in any circumstances at all he might be tempted to use his authority to set up a Pretender.

CHAPTER 4

WESTMINSTER ABBEY

'The Abbey of Westminster hath been always held the greatest sanctuary and randevouze of devotion of the whole island: whereunto the situation of the very place seems to contribute much, and to strike a holy kind of reverence and sweetness of melting piety in the hearts of the beholders.' So wrote James Howell in 1657. For three hundred years since then poets, priests, statesmen and kings have been buried there, and it is now more than ever the central shrine of the English race and people.

There is some evidence that a monastery or church was built on the present site by Sebert, King of the East Saxons who died in the year 616, but the certain foundation of the Abbey dates from the reign of Edward the Confessor, who was in a sense the last of the Saxon and the first of the Norman Kings. He was the son of Ethelred the Unready who vainly tried to appease the Danes with Danegelt. He was brought up in exile in Normandy during the reign of King Canute. While living in Normandy he made a vow that if called to the throne of England he would pay a pilgrimage to the grave of St Peter in Rome and be crowned by the Pope.

A short time later the Danes withdrew from England, and Edward the Confessor was elected King. But when he informed his great Council of the vow he had made they were horrified. The journey to Rome was exceedingly dangerous and he could not leave without their consent. The King gave way when it was suggested that a deputation might be sent to the Pope to ask for release from his vow. The Pope granted him release on condition that he should found or restore a monastery dedicated to St Peter and be the Patron of it himself. That is why the true name of the Abbey as confirmed in the Charter which Queen Elizabeth the First issued after the Reformation is the 'Collegiate Church of Saint Peter in Westminster'.

The Saxon kings had mostly lived in Winchester. Edward started to build his Abbey shortly after he was crowned in 1043. To supervise the building of the Abbey, he began to live at Westminster, and the Abbey and the Palace grew together side by side just as in

Scotland, a few years later, did Dunfermline Palace and Dunfermline Abbey. In his charter Edward wrote: 'destroying the old building I have built up a new one from the very foundation'. It was the first cruciform church in England and was very large for the period, occupying almost the whole area of the present building. The foundations were built of massive blocks of grey stone but the towers were of wood. Of this original structure nothing remains above ground to-day. In 1066 Edward died and was buried in his Abbey ten days after it had been consecrated. His successor Harold was slain at the Battle of Hastings within a few months of his accession and the first coronation that was certainly held on the present site was that of William the Conqueror on Christmas Day, 1066.

The face of England was to be transformed. A few days before the coronation, Norman workmen had been imported to London to lay the foundations of the Tower of London which was to be the central citadel of Norman power. The ancient form of popular election, derived from Teutonic sources, was observed in the coronation service. There was a mixed congregation of Saxons and Normans. When the two Bishops, one in English, the other in French, asked for approval of the crowning of Duke William, a confused babel arose from the bilingual congregation. The Norman soldiers stationed all around the Abbey were alarmed and set fire to the gates and possibly to some of the thatched houses around them. The congregation panicked and streamed from the Abbey; William, trembling from head to foot, was, it is said, left alone in the Abbey with the priests and monks for his coronation service.

In 1161, Henry the Second obtained from Pope Alexander a Papal Bull for the canonisation of Edward the Confessor. Two years later, the bones of Edward were disinterred and moved to a new shrine in the presence of King Henry and Archbishop Thomas Becket. The canonisation of Edward was a great political victory for King Henry. It made the English Royal House the only one which had a Saint among its kings and it also emphasised King Henry's connection with the Saxon dynasty.[1] Henry the Second's grandson, Henry the Third, pulled down the Norman Abbey and rebuilt it much as it is to-day. He completed his rebuilding in 1269 and much of the present structure is therefore nearly seven hundred years old.

[1] The Holy Roman Emperor Henry II had been canonised in 1146 but succession to the Empire was not at this time hereditary. The French King Louis was not canonised till 1297.

The Chapel of Saint Edward became the most sacred spot in the Abbey and round it were clustered the tombs of succeeding kings and queens. Thus, by the end of the thirteenth century, Westminster was firmly established as a national shrine and as the centuries passed its fabric and ornament became a living and growing record of English history.

Thirty years after the Abbey had been rebuilt, King Edward the First invaded Scotland, defeated William Wallace, and brought back the Stone of Scone, which he encased in an oaken chair. The two most important structural additions to the Abbey since the thirteenth-century design of Henry the Third have been the Henry VII Chapel and the twin towers at the west front which were designed by Sir Christopher Wren and executed by Hawksmoor.

From the earliest times the Abbey, which was the home of a Benedictine community, did not form part of any English diocese. Until the Reformation it came directly under the Pope of Rome. When Elizabeth the First came to the throne, the Benedictine Abbey had already been dispossessed by her father, Henry the Eighth, and she issued a new charter which is still in force to-day, by which the Abbey became a 'Royal Peculiar' and she and her successors became the 'Visitors'.

Royal authority over the Abbey does not, therefore, merely arise from the fact that since the Reformation the sovereign has been head of the Church of England. To-day the Dean and Chapter are responsible to no one save the Queen. Her Majesty, like most of her predecessors since Richard the Third in 1483, has required the Earl Marshal, the Duke of Norfolk, to take over the Abbey and prepare it for her coronation.

If all written works were to perish, historians a hundred years hence could piece together a comprehensive history of England from its tombs and monuments which range from that of Edward the Confessor to that of the Unknown Warrior. Macaulay, in a famous passage, has recorded how Englishmen, a hundred years ago, were affected by the historic atmosphere of the Abbey: 'Chatham sleeps near the northern door of the Church, in a spot which has ever since been appropriated to statesmen, as the other end of the same transept has long been to poets; Mansfield rests there, and the second William Pitt, and Fox, and Grattan, and Canning and Wilberforce. In no other cemetery do so many great citizens lie within so narrow a space. High over those venerable graves towers the stately monument of Chatham, and from above, his effigy, graven by a cunning hand, seems still, with eagle face and outstretched arm, to bid England be of good cheer, and to hurl defiance at her foes.'

Twice in our lifetime Britain has profited from the inspiration of Chatham; the Battle of Britain Chapel is only the last of a hundred sacred memorials in the Abbey which tell the tale of the high and unique destiny of our island race.

CHAPTER 5

THE ABBEY CEREMONY

When the Queen arrives at the West door of Westminster Abbey on June 2, she will be received by the Earl Marshal and by other Great Officers of the Realm. Soon after her arrival the procession, which will have been marshalled in the annexe, will move up the Nave while the choir sing Psalm CXXII, 'I was glad when they said unto me we will go into the house of the Lord'. She will be supported on one side by the Bishop of Durham and on the other by the Bishop of Bath and Wells, who have had the right to discharge this privileged duty ever since the Coronation of King Richard I. Immediately in front of the Queen will be carried the coronation regalia. The regalia procession will be made up as shown in Appendix B.

As the Queen passes under the organ loft she will, by ancient tradition, be acclaimed by the Queen's Scholars of Westminster School in the only Latin which is now used in the Coronation Service, 'Vivat Regina Elizabetha! Vivat! Vivat! Vivat!' The Kings and Queens of England have long associations with Westminster School. Queen Elizabeth I was once going round the school when a boy who had recently been birched was pointed out to her. She asked him to recount his experiences. The boy replied in the immortal words which Queen Dido addressed to Aeneas: *Infandum regina jubes renovare dolorem*. 'Too deep for words, O Queen, lies the sorrow thou bidst me renew.'[1]

The coronation ceremony is conducted in what is called the Theatre: the raised platform in the space which Henry III incorporated in his plan for the rebuilding of the Abbey with the special end in view that it might serve for Coronations.

As soon as the Queen has seated herself on the South side of the sanctuary, the Archbishop of Canterbury, with the Earl Marshal and other Great Officers of the Realm, preceded by Garter King of Arms, will walk in turn to the four sides of the Theatre and at

[1] This line is perhaps more exactly rendered in the recent English translation of the Aeneid by Mr C. Day Lewis: 'O Queen, the griefs you bid me reopen are inexpressible.'

each proclaim Queen Elizabeth, 'your undoubted Queen: Wherefore All you who are come this day to do your Homage and Service, Are you willing to do the same ?' Meanwhile the Queen, who will have risen from her chair, will face each side in turn as the congregation reply 'God Save Queen Elizabeth'. This ceremony is known as the Recognition and is a survival from the time when the succession of a sovereign had to be confirmed by the acclamation of the people.

The Recognition is followed by the Oath which is administered to the Queen by the Archbishop of Canterbury. Having answered the questions addressed to her by the Archbishop, the Queen will next go to the Altar, kneel down, lay her hand on the Bible and vow to perform and keep the oath which she has promised. She then signs the Oath with the pen from the silver standish and returns to her chair. All this is merely by way of introduction, and has no sacramental significance. At this point the Bible will be presented to the Queen. Since the reign of William and Mary when this feature was introduced into the service, the Bible has always been presented later in the service with the Regalia. This has long been thought an awkward moment and the change is an undoubted improvement. Another change is that the Moderator of the Church of Scotland is to be associated with the presentation of the Bible. The new form of words is as follows:

> *Archbishop:* Our gracious Queen: to keep your Majesty ever mindful of the law and the gospel of God as the Rule for the whole life and government of Christian Princes, we present you with this Book, the most valuable thing that this world affords.

> *Moderator:* Here is wisdom; this is the royal law; these are the lively Oracles of God.

All else that follows in the ceremony of coronation is enshrined in the Communion Service with which the ceremony ends.

The next part of the Service is concerned with the preparation of the Queen prior to her being anointed and receiving the Royal unction. The later Plantagenets and the Tudors knelt to be anointed. Charles I was anointed sitting and all English sovereigns since then have followed his example. After a number of prayers and the reciting of the Litany, there is a prayer to consecrate the oil in the Ampulla with which the Queen will be anointed. The Queen, who will have arrived in a crimson robe of state, will now discard it, while the choir sing the hymn VENI CREATOR, 'Come Holy Ghost, our souls inspire'.

The Archbishop, assisted by the Dean of Westminster, will then anoint the Queen on the hands and the breast and the crown of her head.[1] The Archbishop pronounces as he does so: 'And as Solomon was anointed King by Zadok the priest and Nathan the prophet, so be you anointed, blessed and consecrated Queen over the Peoples, whom the Lord your God hath given you to rule and govern . . .'

While the choir sing the eighth-century anthem 'Zadok the Priest' which, since the coronation of George II, has always been sung to Handel's music, the Queen will be invested with the Colobium Sindonis which is a sleeveless garment and then with the Supertunica of cloth of gold, lined with crimson silk, together with its girdle or sword belt.

The rest of the regalia, which have already been blessed, will now be handed to the Queen. First come the Spurs. The Dean brings them from the Altar and hands them to the Lord Great Chamberlain, Lord Cholmondeley, who will present them to the Queen. Her Majesty will touch them and they will then be returned to the Altar. The Archbishop then lays the Sword on the Altar and afterwards hands it to the Queen with the words: 'Do justice, stop the growth of iniquity, protect the Holy Church of God, help and defend widows and orphans, restore the things which are gone to decay, maintain the things that are restored, punish and reform what is amiss, and confirm what is in good order.'

In the case of a King, the Sword would then be girded, but the Queen will follow the precedent of Queen Victoria and hold it in her hand and offer it at the Altar. When she returns to her chair she will be invested with the Armill (which are bracelets not used since the Coronation of Edward VI), the Stole, and then with the Pallium of cloth of gold.

Next the Queen must be handed the other regalia: first the Orb with the Cross, the symbol of worldly power; 'Receive this Orb', pronounces the Archbishop, 'set under the Cross, and remember that the whole world is subject to the Power and Empire of Christ our Redeemer.'

Next comes the Ring, 'the ensign of kingly dignity'; then the Sceptre with the Cross, symbolising all kingly power and justice, and then the Rod with the Dove, symbolical of 'Equity and Mercy'. Everything is now ready for the actual crowning.

[1] Since 1682 Kings have been anointed on the head, the breast and the hands. At Queen Victoria's Coronation anointing on the breast was omitted 'from motives of delicacy'.

Taking the crown of St Edward from the Altar where it was placed at the beginning of the Service, the Archbishop will recite the following prayer:

O God, the crown of the faithful: Bless we beseech thee and sanctify this thy servant Elizabeth our Queen: and as thou dost this day set a Crown of pure gold upon her head, so enrich her royal heart with thine abundant grace, and crown her with all princely virtues, through the King eternal, Jesus Christ our Lord. Amen.

The Queen meanwhile will be seated in St Edward's chair. The Archbishop, assisted by other Bishops, will now come from the Altar. The Dean of Westminster will bring the Crown and, in the words of the rubric,

. . . the Archbishop taking it of him shall reverently put it upon the Queen's head. At the sight whereof the people, with loud and repeated shouts, shall cry, GOD SAVE THE QUEEN; the Peers and the Kings of Arms shall put on their coronets[1]; and the trumpets shall sound, and, by a signal given, the great guns at the Tower shall be shot off.

When the acclamation has died down the Archbishop will pronounce these words:

God crown you with a crown of glory and righteousness, that by the ministry of this our benediction, having a right faith and manifold fruit of good works, you may obtain the crown of an everlasting kingdom by the gift of him whose kingdom endureth for ever. Amen.

'And now', the rubric continues, 'the Queen having been thus anointed and crowned, and having received all the ensigns of royalty, the Archbishop shall solemnly bless her: and the Archbishop of York and all the Bishops, with the rest of the Peers, shall follow every part of the Benediction with a loud and hearty Amen.'

The Benediction formerly concluded with the words:

The Lord give you fruitful lands and healthful seasons; victorious fleets and armies, and a quiet Empire: a faithful Senate, wise and upright counsellors and magistrates, a loyal nobility, and a dutiful gentry; a pious and learned and useful clergy; an honest, peaceable, and obedient commonalty.

No doubt this noble period piece of Archbishop Sancroft with its reference to a 'peaceable and obedient commonalty' would be thought out of place in the age of the cosh; this part of the rubric has therefore been replaced with the following words:

The Lord give you faithful Parliaments and quiet Realms; sure

[1] In the case of a King's Coronation the peeresses do not put on their coronets until the Queen is crowned. This year the peeresses will put on their coronets at the same time as the peers.

The Coronation of King Henry III by Peter, Bishop of Winchester, and Joceline, Bishop of Bath

defence against all enemies; fruitful lands and a prosperous industry; wise counsellors and upright magistrates; leaders of integrity in learning and labour; a devout, learned and useful clergy; honest, peaceable and dutiful citizens. May Wisdom and Knowledge be the Stability of your Times, and the Fear of the Lord your Treasure.

There follows the enthronement: the rubric continues:

> Then shall the Queen go to her throne, and be lifted up into it by the Archbishops and Bishops, and other Peers of the Kingdom; and being Inthronised, or placed therein, all the Great Officers, those that bear the Swords and Sceptres, and the Nobles who carried the other Regalia, shall stand round about the steps of the throne; and the Archbishop standing before the Queen shall say:

> 'Stand firm and hold fast from henceforth the seat and state of royal and imperial dignity, which is this day delivered unto you, in the Name and by the authority of Almighty God, and by the hands of us the Bishops and servants of God, though unworthy' . . .

This exhortation ended, there follows the Homage. According to ancient tradition the Archbishop of Canterbury is the first to do fealty.[1]   However, in 1702, at the last Coronation where a Sovereign Queen was already married, Prince George of Denmark appears to have done homage as Duke of Cumberland to Queen Anne before the Lords Spiritual. This year the older traditional pre-eminence of the Archbishop will be maintained. The Archbishop will, at the appointed moment, kneel down before Her Majesty while the rest of the Bishops kneel in their places. The Bishops repeating after him, the Archbishop will say:

> I, Geoffrey Archbishop of Canterbury will be faithful and true, and faith and truth will bear unto you our Sovereign Lady of this Realm and Queen, Defender of the Faith . . .

The Archbishop then salutes the Queen with a kiss on the hand. Thereafter the Duke of Edinburgh, the Duke of Gloucester and the Duke of Kent take off their coronets and kneel in turn before her and

> arising severally touch the crown on her Majesty's head and kiss her Majesty's left cheek . . . the other Peers of the Realm, who are then in their seats, shall kneel down, put off their Coronets, and do their Homage, the Dukes first by themselves, and so the Marquesses, the Earls, the Viscounts, and the Barons, severally in their places . . .

The Homage will be pronounced for the Dukes by the Duke of Norfolk, for the Marquesses by Lord Huntly (the senior Marquess, Lord Winchester, being unable to attend), for the Earls

---

[1] The Lords spiritual do fealty, the Lords temporal, homage.

by Lord Shrewsbury, for the Viscounts by Lord Falkland (in the absence of Viscount Hereford who is not quite twenty-one and therefore a minor), for the Barons by Lord Mowbray and Stourton. Meanwhile the choir will sing a number of anthems:

'Rejoice in the Lord always.'
'O clap your hands together, all ye people.'
'I will not leave thee comfortless.'
'O Lord our Governor.'
'Thou will keep him in perfect peace, whose mind is stayed on Thee.'

When the Homage is ended, 'the drums shall beat, and the trumpets sound, and all the people shout, crying out:

"God save Queen ELIZABETH
Long live Queen ELIZABETH
May the Queen live for ever" '.

In former times, while the fealty and homage were being done, the Treasurer of the Household, Garter King of Arms and Black Rod scattered medals of gold and silver among the congregation from the four sides of the stage. Pepys in his *Diary* describes this ancient ceremony at the Coronation of Charles II: 'And a Generall Pardon also was read by the Lord Chancellor, and meddalls flung up and down by my Lord Cornwallis, of silver, but I could not come by any.' The General Pardon seems to have been omitted since the Coronation of George II.

This completes the crowning and all that remains is the Communion Service. Until the coronation of George III, in 1761, English Sovereigns had always taken Holy Communion wearing their crowns. In those days the arrangements were not so carefully planned as nowadays, nor were there any rehearsals. When George III was about to receive Communion he asked Archbishop Secker, who had baptised, confirmed, married and now crowned him, whether he should remove his crown. The Archbishop consulted with the Dean (Zachary Pearce) but they could not recall any precedent. 'Then there ought to be one', said the King removing his crown. He urged the Queen to do the same, but her crown was pinned to her hair and she could not do so. Since then his sensible example has been followed, and the rubric this year will read almost as it did for Queen Victoria:

The Queen descends from Her Throne, attended by Her Supporters, and assisted by the Lord Great Chamberlain, the Sword of State being carried before Her, and goes to the Steps of the Altar, where, taking off Her Crown, which She delivers to the Lord Great Chamberlain to hold, She kneels down.

34

At this point there will be a collect and a blessing for the Duke of Edinburgh, who will receive Communion with the Queen. The Communion Service completed, there follows the Recess. The Queen, carrying the Sceptre and the Rod, attended and accompanied as on her entry into the Abbey, with the four Swords carried before her, will descend from the throne and, passing through the choir on the South side of the Abbey, will come into St Edward's Chapel. As the procession passes the Altar, the rest of the regalia will be delivered by the Dean of Westminster to the Great Officers of the Realm and other peers who carried them into the Abbey. The Queen will then be disrobed of her golden robe and will be arrayed in a robe of purple velvet. Here the Queen will remove the Crown of St Edward and replace it with the Imperial Crown which weighs much less, the Crown of St Edward not being used again until the next Coronation.

Then the Queen, carrying the Orb in her left hand and the Sceptre with the cross in her right, will proceed through the choir to the West door of the Abbey by which she came in and after an interval while the procession is being formed will enter the State Coach with the Duke of Edinburgh for the almost two-hour return drive to Buckingham Palace.

CHAPTER 6

THE REGALIA

Very little remains of the ancient Regalia of England. In 1643 Charles I, embarrassed by lack of funds, is believed to have had one of his crowns and one of his sceptres melted down and minted into money. And in 1649 the House of Commons, at Cromwell's directions, ordered the complete destruction of the Regalia which was then in the custody of Sir Harry Mildmay, afterwards known as 'the knave of diamonds'.[1] The Commons ordered that the Regalia should be delivered to the 'trustees for the sale of the goods of the late king, who are to cause the same to be totally broken, and that they melt down all the gold and silver, and sell the jewels to the best advantage of the Commonwealth'.

When Charles II was restored to the throne in 1660 it was, therefore, necessary to provide new Regalia. Sir Robert Vyner, the King's Goldsmith, was entrusted with this task. For the sum of £31,978 9s 11d Vyner produced two crowns, two sceptres, an orb 'of gold sett with diamonds, rubies, saphires, emeralds, and pearls', 'St. Edward's staffe', 'The Armilla' and 'The Ampull'.

The treble character of the Sovereign – priestly, military and governmental – is illustrated by the nature of the Regalia. The priestly element greatly predominates. The Colobium Sindonis, the Dalmatic and the Mantle all have their ecclesiastical equivalents. The Sceptre corresponds to the Crozier and the Crown to the Mitre. All these Regalia can be shown to have their equivalents in the consecration of a bishop. And we have already seen the similarity between the anointing of a King and a bishop. The military and chivalric emblems are the Sword and Spurs. Some authorities hold that the Orb appears to be the sole symbol of Christian Dominion and independent Christian sovereignty and that it illustrates the Queen's role as a ruler rather than as a priest or soldier.

---

[1] Mildmay owed this nickname to a curious codicil added to the Will of the Earl of Pembroke, who died in the following year, which ran as follows:

'Because I threatened Sir Harry Mildmay but did not beat him, I give fifty pounds to the footman who cudgelled him. Item, my will is that the said Sir Harry shall not meddle with my jewells. I knew him when he served the Duke of Buckingham and, since, how he handled the crowne jewells, for both which reasons I now name him the *knave of diamonds*.'

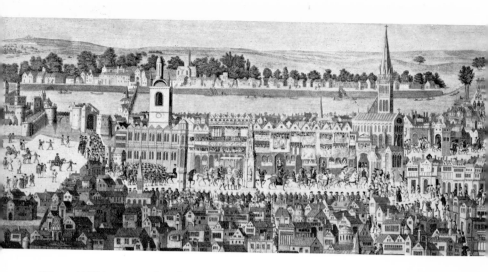

Edward VI in procession from the Tower of London to Westminster on the eve of his Coronation

Detail from above showing Cheapside Cross

Drawn by Mr. Chambers.   Engravd by W. Thom

The Inside of Henry the 7ths Chapel in

In Appendix C will be found a complete list of all the Regalia which is to-day kept in the Jewel House at the Tower of London. Here I shall merely describe that part of the Regalia which is actually used in the coronation.

The Royal Vestments which are used at coronations are part of the Regalia. They are four in number:

> Colobium Sindonis,
> Dalmatic, and Girdle,
> Stole,
> Imperial Mantle.

THE COLOBIUM SINDONIS is the first garment that will be put upon the Queen after the anointing. It represents the alb of a priest, or the rochet of a bishop. It is a sleeveless garment of fine linen cambric with a lace border. It is open at the side and cut low at the neck and is edged all round with lace. It is gathered in at the waist and open on the left shoulder. It is fastened with three small buttons and there are three sham buttons to match on the right. A new one is being made for the Queen.

THE DALMATIC, OR SUPERTUNICA, is put on after the Colobium Sindonis. A dalmatic is a religious vestment imitated from the national dress of Dalmatia. It is a long coat of cloth of gold with wide sleeves. The edges are trimmed with gold lace. It has a pattern of green palm leaves interspersed with pink roses, green shamrocks and purple thistles. The design is worked in very pale colours and is of great beauty. It is lined with rose-coloured silk.

THE STOLE is a band of cloth of gold, 3 inches wide and about 5 feet long, with a bullion fringe at each end. It is heavily embroidered with gold and silver thread and at either end there is a square panel worked with the red cross of St George on a silver background. Like the Dalmatic, it is lined with rose-coloured silk. A new one is being designed for the Queen.

THE PALL OR IMPERIAL MANTLE is the last garment to be put upon the Queen. The Pall is similar in design to the Cope worn by a bishop. Queen Victoria's Mantle, which can be seen in the London Museum, is 5 inches in depth and measures 28 inches across the shoulders. It has a gold bullion fringe $2\frac{1}{2}$ inches long and is also lined with rose-coloured silk. It is worked in a pattern of silver coronets and fleurs-de-lys with green leaves, shamrocks and purple and green thistles and silver eagles in between.

THE ORB WITH THE CROSS is 6 inches in diameter and is a very ancient Christian ornament. Some of the later Roman Emperors used them and the early Saxon kings adopted the emblem from them. The Orb with the Cross is the oldest emblem of Christian sovereignty. In the British Museum there is a very fine carved ivory diptych of the early sixth century showing the Archangel Michael holding in his hand an orb with a cross, very similar to that found on the Great Seal of Queen Elizabeth I. The Orb which will be used at this coronation was made for Charles II. On it is a jewelled cross set in a base of amethyst.

TWO SCEPTRES will next be handed to the Queen, the Sceptre with the cross and the Sceptre with the dove. The former is made of gold and is 36 inches long. It contains the largest portion of the Cullinan diamond, weighing 500 carats. This diamond is $2\frac{1}{2}$ inches long and has adorned the royal sceptre since the reign of King Edward VII. The Sceptre with the dove is also made of gold and is 41 inches long. The dove, which is of gold and white enamel, is symbolic of the Holy Ghost and signifies Equity and Mercy.

Dean Stanley, a famous Dean of Westminster in the middle of the last century, further expressed the view that the dove 'was the reminiscence of St Edward's peaceful days after the expulsion of the Danes'.

TWO CROWNS will be used at the coronation. The Queen will be crowned with *St Edward's Crown*, but she will only wear it for a short time as it weighs over $4\frac{1}{2}$ lb. Instead she will then wear the Imperial State Crown which was made for Queen Victoria as it was thought that St Edward's Crown 'was too large for her small girlish head'. Like all the rest of the regalia, with the exception of the Spoon and possibly the Ampulla, the Crown of St Edward was made for Charles II's coronation in 1661.

St Edward's Crown is always carried in the coronation procession by the Lord High Steward. Inside the Crown is the Cap of Maintenance which is of purple velvet edged with miniver. The rim of the Crown is set with gems and from it spring two gold arches which are the actual symbols of sovereignty. Where the arches meet there is a gold orb surmounted by a jewelled cross.

THE IMPERIAL STATE CROWN is not so historic as St Edward's Crown but is far more valuable. The present one was made for Queen Victoria in 1838 and contains the Black Prince's ruby. It also contains the second largest portion of the Cullinan diamond weighing 300 carats. In the centre of the cross at the top of the Crown is the sapphire which is supposed to have belonged to Edward the Confessor and there are four large drop pearls which may once have belonged to Queen Elizabeth I. In the back of the Crown there is also set the famous oval Stuart sapphire which James II took with him into exile. Whereas the Queen will never after her coronation wear the Crown of St Edward again, she will continue to use the Imperial State Crown whenever she opens Parliament in State.

ST EDWARD'S STAFF is probably the only one of the Regalia made by Sir Robert Vyner for Charles II which is still in exactly the same condition as when it was made. It is 4 feet 7½ inches long and is made of gold with collars of ornamental leaf patterns. It has a steel tip 4 inches long and was originally supposed to be a staff to guide the footsteps of the King. But for several hundreds of years it has always been carried by a peer who is invited by the Sovereign to have this honour.

THE SPURS. The pair of golden spurs are of solid gold, elaborately chased and enamelled and with straps of crimson velvet embroidered in gold. They are known as St George's Spurs and are emblems of Knighthood and Chivalry. They are what are called 'prick' spurs as, instead of ending in a rowel, they have a sharp point.

THE CHALICE is made of solid gold engraved with the royal coat of arms. It is used for Holy Communion after the crowning.

THE SWORDS. Five swords will be used in the Coronation:
   (1) Sword of State.
   (2) Sword Spiritual ('Sword of Justice to the Spirituality').
   (3) Sword Temporal ('Sword of Justice to the Temporality').
   (4) Curtana or Sword of Mercy.
   (5) The Queen's Jewelled Sword.

1. THE SWORD OF STATE is a two-handed sword and is the largest one in the Regalia. The Queen may entrust any of her subjects with the carrying of the Sword, which is one of the most honourable functions in the coronation. In 1937 it was carried by the Marquess of Zetland. This year it is to be carried by the Marquess of Salisbury. At the coronation of George III the Earl Marshal forgot the Sword of State and at the last moment borrowed

one from the Lord Mayor of London. The King complained of this oversight to Lord Effingham, the Deputy Earl Marshal, who replied 'It is true sir; but I have taken care that the next coronation shall be regulated in the exactest manner possible.' This was not thought a tactful answer. George III reigned for sixty-three years and Lord Effingham was no longer available to carry out his promise – he had been dead for thirty years when George IV was crowned.

2 AND 3. THE SWORDS SPIRITUAL AND TEMPORAL are less magnificent than the Sword of State and very similar to each other. They will be carried by the Earl of Home and the Duke of Buccleuch.

4. THE SWORD OF MERCY KNOWN AS CURTANA has a blunted end and resembles the Swords Temporal and Spiritual. Three such swords were presented to Henry VIII by the Pope at the same time that the latter made the King Defender of the Faith.

5. THE QUEEN'S JEWELLED STATE SWORD is far the most elaborate of the Swords. It was specially made for the Coronation of King George IV and cost £6,000 in the money of those days. It is this Sword which the Queen will offer at the Altar during the Coronation Service. After she has offered it at the Altar it will be redeemed for one hundred shillings, and drawn from its scabard and carried naked and with the point upward during the rest of the service, by the bearer of the Sword of State – which is then placed in St Edward's Chapel.

THE AMPULLA is a golden eagle from which is poured the oil with which Sovereigns are anointed. It is of solid gold and weighs about ten ounces. It can hold about six ounces of oil. The head unscrews so that the oil can be introduced and it pours out through the beak. It is about 9 inches high. It almost certainly ante-dates nearly all the rest of the Regalia though it is probable that Charles II's jeweller, Sir Robert Vyner, had to make very considerable repairs to it.

THE SPOON. Like the Ampulla, the spoon into which the oil is poured is of considerable antiquity, probably dating from the twelfth century. It is made of silver, very heavily gilt and the bowl of the spoon, which is probably not as old as the handle and may have been remade by Sir Robert Vyner, has a ridge down the middle. It is thought that the Abbey authorities may have managed to conceal the Spoon and Ampulla as being particularly Holy, when the Cromwellians removed the rest of the Regalia to the Tower in 1649.

THE RING. Usually English Kings and Queens have had Coronation Rings specially made for them and retained them as their own private property. The Queen will probably use one of the three existing rings. The finest of the Coronation Rings is made with a sapphire and rubies in the form of the cross of St George. The ring symbolises the union of the Sovereign and the people. Dean Stanley said of it 'The ring with which, as the Doge to the Adriatic, so the King to his people was wedded, was the ring of the pilgrim.'

PART II

CHAPTER 7

QUEEN MARY I

When King Edward VI died at Greenwich Palace in July 1553 at the age of sixteen, he left a will by which he disinherited his two sisters, the Princess Mary and the Princess Elizabeth. In this will, which was certainly illegal, he bestowed the Crown upon his cousin, Lady Jane Gray. She had recently married Lord Guildford Dudley, the youngest son of the Regent, the Duke of Northumberland. Immediately upon the King's death Northumberland proclaimed Lady Jane Gray as Queen.

The adherents of Lady Jane Gray sought to trap Princess Mary by concealing the death of the King and luring her to London on the pretext that he was ill. But Mary was warned in time and took refuge at Framlingham Castle in Suffolk where she forthwith displayed her standard over the gate-tower and assumed the title of Queen-regnant of England and Ireland. The country as a whole rallied to Mary's cause and the Northumberland faction soon melted away. Despite Mary's desire in this case to be merciful, Lady Jane Gray was condemned by a Bill of Attainder shortly after the coronation 'to be burned on Tower Hill or beheaded at the Queen's pleasure'. It was believed that Mary would pardon her cousin who was an innocent victim of the ambitions of others; but this was not to be.

Shortly after her coronation the Queen announced her engagement (which she had already secretly entered into some weeks before) to Philip II of Spain. Within a week three insurrections broke out in different parts of England. One in the West of England led by Sir Peter Carew had the intention of placing the Earl of Devonshire and Princess Elizabeth on the throne; the second, which was the most considerable, was headed by Sir Thomas Wyatt; the third, organised in the Midlands by the vassals of the Duke of Suffolk, aimed at the restoration of Lady Jane Gray. These events proved decisive for the unfortunate Lady Jane and she was almost immediately beheaded.

Mary was the first Queen-regnant to come to the Throne of England. She was thirty-seven. There might have been opposition to a woman reigning but for the extraordinary fact that all her nearest heirs were also women. There being no precedents for the coronation of a Queen-regnant, it was decided that it should be managed in 'all particulars like unto the King of England'. The chief embarrassment of the time was, however, the lack of money. There was not one penny in the Royal purse and the Queen was forced to borrow £20,000 in the City of London before she could be crowned.

Next only to the lack of money was felt the lack of Bishops to perform the ceremony. Cranmer, Archbishop of Canterbury, Latimer, Bishop of Worcester, and Ridley, Bishop of London, were held in the Tower for their Protestant faith for which three years later they were to go to the stake. The duty had, therefore, to be entrusted to Stephen Gardiner, Bishop of Winchester.

In the distressed and confused state of the realm it was thought desirable for the coronation to take place as soon as possible. It was fixed for October 1, less than three months after the death of Edward VI. Three days before the coronation, the Queen moved from St James's to Whitehall. Thence, accompanied by her sister, Princess Elizabeth, and the ladies of the Court, she proceeded by barge to the Tower escorted by other barges with the Lord Mayor and Livery Companies with 'streamers, trumpets, waits, shawms, and regals'.

The next day, according to the custom which had begun in 1399 with the reign of Henry IV, she made fifteen Knights of the Bath. She did not dub them herself but delegated the task to the Lord Steward, Henry Earl of Arundel, who knighted them in her presence. The following day in the afternoon the Queen went in procession through the streets of the City of London. Seventy ladies clad in crimson velvet rode behind the Queen on horseback and five hundred gentlemen, noblemen and ambassadors walked before her. The Queen sat in a litter supported by six white horses and covered with a cloth of silver. She wore a gown of blue velvet trimmed with ermine. On her head she wore a heavy and valuable gold circlet set with pearls and precious gems. Her sister Elizabeth rode behind her in 'an open chariot richly covered with crimson velvet'. By her side sat Anne of Cleves, the surviving widow of her father, Henry VIII.

Much pageantry marked the Queen's progress through the City.

44

MARIE.

In Fenchurch Street she halted while speeches were recited by 'four great giants'. In Gracechurch Street she was regaled with 'a solo on the trumpet, from a great angel in green, perched on a triumphal arch prepared by the Florentine merchants'. Wine ran freely in Cornhill and Cheapside and the aldermen of the latter presented the Queen with '1000 marks in a crimson purse'. At St Paul's School the Queen's favourite poet and player, Heywood, sat under a vine and delivered an oration. The procession ended at the Palace of Whitehall.

On the next morning, October 1, the Queen and her suite once more embarked in their barges and landed at the stairs of the old Palace of Westminster. Here she was conducted to a private apartment where she was robed. The procession from Westminster Hall to the Abbey began about 11 o'clock. The Queen, dressed in her crimson Parliament robes, walked under the traditional canopy carried by the Barons of the Cinque Ports. Her train was borne by the Duchess of Norfolk, attended by the Vice-Chamberlain, Sir John Gage. Immediately behind the Queen walked the Princess Elizabeth, followed by Anne of Cleves.

The choir of Westminster Abbey was hung with tapestries and the floor was strewn with rushes. The Queen was supported on her right by the Bishop of Durham and on her left by the Earl of Shrewsbury.[1] When they had conducted her to St Edward's Chair the Bishop of Winchester proceeded to the ceremony of Recognition and addressed her in words which were more comprehensive than any used before:

> Sirs, Here present is Mary, rightful and undoubted inheritrix, by the laws of God and man, to the crown and royal dignity of this realm of England, France, and Ireland; and you shall understand, that this day is appointed by all the peers of this land for the consecration, unction, and coronation of the said most excellent princess Mary. Will you serve at this time, and give your wills and assent to the same consecration, unction, and coronation?

The congregation replied: 'Yea, yea, yea! God save Queen Mary!' After the administration of the oath and the reading of the Litany, the Queen was led to her traverse on the left hand of the altar and 'there was unarrayed and unclothed' by her ladies of the privy-chamber. After she had been anointed she retired once more to the traverse and returned 'in a robe of white taffeta, and a mantle of purple velvet furred with ermine'. She was then seated in a chair

---

[1] This seems to be one of the few occasions on which the second supporter was not the Bishop of Bath and Wells.

near the altar and the Duke of Norfolk brought to her three crowns, St Edward's crown, the Imperial crown of England and a third crown which had been made expressly for her. She was successively crowned with all three. There is no record of the significance of the third crown, but it has been surmised that it may have represented the kingdom of Ireland.

Having been invested with all the royal garments and regalia, she was brought to St Edward's Chair for the homage. The Queen 'sat apparelled in her royal robes of velvet, – a mantle with a train; a surcoat, with a kirtle furred with wombs of miniver pure; a riband of Venice gold; a mangle-lace [cordon] of silk and gold, with buttons and tassels of the same, having the crown imperial on her head, her sceptre in her right hand, and the orb in her left, and a pair of sabatons on her feet covered with crimson cloth of gold, garnished with riband of Venice gold, delivered to her by her master of the great wardrobe'.

The Duke of Norfolk was the first after the bishops to do homage with the words:

> I become your liege man of life and limb, and of all earthly worship and faith, and all truly shall bear unto you, to live and die with you against all manner of folk. God so help me and All-hallows!

When all the peers, who in those days numbered no more than fifty, had paid homage they all cried: 'God save Queen Mary!' Her brother Edward VI whom she succeeded had been a Protestant. Mary refused to use for her crowning the same chair that he had used, since she considered that it had been polluted by a heretic. She used instead a chair which was specially sent from Rome by the Pope. It is now preserved in the Cathedral at Winchester. It was significant that, though she sat in St Edward's Chair when she first entered the Abbey and sat there again for the homage, she was actually crowned in the Papal Chair.

At Edward VI's Coronation in 1546, the Mass had been greatly abridged partly 'for the tedious length of the same, and the tender age of the King' and partly 'for that many points of the same were such as by the laws of the nation were not allowable'. Mary insisted on the full ceremony being restored and, thinking that the Ampulla might have lost its virtue as a result of the Papal interdict, she had procured fresh oil from France which had been blessed by the Bishop of Arras.

The General Pardon was still a part of the coronation service but, as one historian has written, it 'contained so many exceptions, that it seemed more like a general accusation, and bore melancholy evidence to the convulsive state of the times'. The ceremony concluded, the Queen processed back to Whitehall for the banquet. Princess Elizabeth, as heiress-presumptive to the throne, was treated with marked respect and was placed at the Queen's left hand with Anne of Cleves beyond her. These 'virgin princes', as the historian and cartographer John Speed calls Mary and Elizabeth, were chaperoned by their father's surviving widow whom both treated with dutiful respect.

The Queen's Champion, Sir Edward Dymoke, rode into the Hall in full armour and pronounced for the first time on behalf of a Queen-regnant the traditional challenge:

> If there be any manner of man, of whatever estate, degree, or condition soever he be, that will say and maintain that our sovereign lady, queen Mary the First, this day here present, is not the rightful and undoubted inheritrix to the imperial crown of this realm of England, and that of right she ought not to be crowned queen, I say he lieth like a false traitor! and that I am ready the same to maintain with him while I have breath in my body, either now at this time, or any other whensoever it shall please the queen's highness to appoint ; and therefore I cast him my gage.

No one took up the challenge though, with adherents of both Lady Jane Gray and Princess Elizabeth in the hall, there was probably a greater chance of this happening than at any other coronation.

Garter King of Arms made the three traditional obeisances before the Queen at the upper end of the hall in Latin, French and English and proclaimed the styles and titles:

> Of the most high, puissant, and most excellent princess, Mary the First, by the grace of God queen of England, France, and Ireland, defender of the faith, of the church of England and Ireland supreme head. Largess, largess, largess!

At the conclusion of the banquet, surrounded by Princess Elizabeth, Anne of Cleves and the nobility, she summoned the foreign ambassadors to her. After talking with them for a short time, she retired, divested herself of her robes and returned by barge to Whitehall where the evening concluded with 'feasting and royal cheer'. Thus ended the coronation of the first Queen-regnant whose short but savage reign was to earn her the name of 'Bloody Mary'.

CHAPTER 8

QUEEN ELIZABETH I

Queen Mary I died on 17 November 1558. Religious dissension divided the land and while Queen Mary lay dying an atmosphere of crisis darkened the capital. The temper of public opinion was well described by Thomas Godwin, later Bishop of Bath and Wells, writing at the time: 'The rich were fearful, the wise careful, the honestly-disposed doubtful, the discontented and desperate were joyful, wishing for strife as the door for plunder.' The Archbishop of York, Dr Heath, who had become Lord Chancellor three years before on the death of Bishop Gardiner, lost no time. Before noon on the day of Mary's death he had summoned the House of Commons to the House of Lords and had proclaimed Elizabeth before the joint assembly.

Elizabeth had had a troubled and perilous youth. When she was only three her father, Henry VIII, had, in the interest of his son (later Edward VI), promoted an Act of Parliament which proclaimed her a bastard. She was now twenty-five. Four years earlier, at the time of Wyatt's Rebellion, she had been imprisoned in the Tower and later at Woodstock for many months. More than once she had nearly suffered the fate of Lady Jane Gray. On one occasion Mary's first Lord Chancellor, Stephen Gardiner, Bishop of Worcester, without consulting the Queen, sent a Privy Council Warrant to the Lieutenant of the Tower ordering her immediate execution. Fortunately the Lieutenant of the Tower, noticing that the Queen's signature was not attached to the Warrant, refused to execute the heiress to the throne 'till he had ascertained the Queen's pleasure'.

Many years later Elizabeth, discussing the perils of her youth with the French Ambassador, Castlenau, said:

that she was in great danger of losing her life from the displeasure her sister had conceived against her, in consequence of the accusations that were fabricated, on the subject of her correspondence with the king of France; and having no hope of escaping, she desired to make her sister only one request, which was, that she might have her head cut off with a sword, as in France, and not with an axe, after the present fashion adopted in England, and therefore desired that an executioner might be sent for out of France, if it were so determined.

48

Elizabeth was a Protestant, but during her sister's reign she had to hide her faith and pay lip-service to the Church of Rome. Camden tells us that during her imprisonment at Woodstock 'the princess Elizabeth, guiding herself like a ship in tempestuous weather, heard divine service after the Romish manner, was frequently confessed, and at the pressing instances of Cardinal Pole, and for fear of death, professed herself to be of the Roman Catholic religion'. In the course of her interrogations by the Catholic Bishops, Elizabeth became a skilful dialectician. Once, when her sister caused her to be questioned as to her belief in the 'real presence of the Saviour in the sacrament' she gave her celebrated reply:

> Christ was the word that spake it,
> He took the bread and brake it,
> And what his word did make it,
> That I believe, and take it.

Elizabeth was at Hatfield when Queen Mary died and it was there that she held her first Privy Council on November 20. Three days later she came to London in procession and all the notabilities of the capital came out to meet her. The Bishops knelt in the road near Highgate and offered their allegiance. She extended her hand to be kissed by all of them except Edmund Bonner, Bishop of London, whose cruelties in the previous reign had been exceptional.

The weakness of Elizabeth's position at the outset of her reign is vividly illustrated by the proceedings at the funeral of the dead Queen in Westminster Abbey. Dr White, Bishop of Winchester, delivered his celebrated 'black sermon'. Mary had renounced the Sovereign's claim to church supremacy established by Henry VIII and Elizabeth was known to be about to reimpose it. Dr White quoted with approval Queen Mary's argument 'that as Saint Paul forbade women to speak in the church, it was not fitting, for the church to have a dumb head'. He remembered 'that queen Mary had left a sister, a lady of greath worth, also, whom they were bound to obey for . . . a living dog is better than a dead lion'. He added 'that the dead deserved more praise, than the living for "Mary had chosen the better part" '. The sermon was preached in Latin; however Elizabeth was an excellent scholar as well as a Tudor and had him arrested as he descended the pulpit stairs. He was deprived of his bishopric and imprisoned in the Tower for a short time, but was soon released as Elizabeth did not wish to gratify his well-advertised desire for public matyrdom. This was robust and sagacious conduct in a girl of twenty-five.

Queen Elizabeth I. This picture, attributed to Gwilym Stretes, is at Warwick Castle

In the weeks before her coronation Elizabeth prepared the ground for her ultimate break with Rome. On the morning of Christmas Day she took the important step of personal secession from the Mass. Surrounded by her household, she attended morning service 'in her closet'. Oglethorpe, Bishop of Carlisle, was at the altar preparing to officiate at High Mass. When, at the end of the Gospel the Queen should have made the usual offering, she rose abruptly and, followed by her retinue, withdrew into her privy chamber. Finding that this action was well received by her subjects, a few days later she issued a proclamation 'that from the approaching new year's day, the litany should, with the epistle and gospel, be said in English in her chapel, and in all churches'.

While anxious to break with 'Romish superstitions', Elizabeth had superstitions of her own and these she respected in fixing the date of her coronation. As in her sister's case, it was desirable that she should be quickly crowned but, before deciding on the date, she sent her Master of the Horse, Lord Robert Dudley, soon to be created Earl of Leicester, 'to consult her pet conjuror, Dr Dee' so that a lucky day might be selected. Guided by Dr Dee, the Queen and her Privy Council chose Sunday, 15 January 1559 as the day likely to be auspicious for the ceremony.

Two days before her coronation, the Queen went by water from the Palace of Westminster to the Tower of London. The Corporation of the City of London and the great livery companies turned out in their State barges 'decked and trimmed with targets and banners of their misteries' and accompanied the Queen to the Tower. An ancient chronicler reported that 'the bachelor's barge of the Lord-mayor's company, to wit the mercers, had their barge with a foist trimmed with three tops, and artillery aboard, gallantly appointed to wait upon them; shooting off lustily as they went with great and pleasant melody of instruments, which played in most sweet and heavenly manner'.

On the day of the coronation the Queen processed from the Tower to Westminster through the City of London. At numerous points on the route triumphal arches had been erected and pageants illustrative of English history were performed. A child was stationed by each arch who recited poems explaining the meaning of the pageant. One pageant exhibited 'a seemly and mete personage, richly apparelled in parliament robes, with sceptre in her hand, over whose head was written: "Deborah, the judge and restorer of the house of Israel." ' The Queen greatly impressed her subjects by the felicitous way in which she spoke to one and all in both Latin and English.

The coronation was conducted by Oglethorpe, Bishop of Carlisle, since the see of Canterbury was vacant, Archbishop Heath of York refused to officiate, and Bonner, Bishop of London, was in prison. On arrival at the Abbey, Elizabeth put on the robes in which she afterwards opened Parliament 'a mantle of crimson velvet, furred with ermine, with a cordon of silk and gold, with buttons and tassels of the same; a train and surcoat of the same velvet, the train and skirt furred with ermine; a cap of maintenance, striped with passaments of gold lace, and a tassel of gold to the same'.

For the most part the ceremony followed the traditional form. The Queen, however, did what she could to agitate for the changes she meant to impose. While Oglethorpe, who was wearing the absent and imprisoned Bishop Bonner's vestments, was kneeling before the altar, the Queen sent him a small book. At first Oglethorpe refused to take it and continued to read the service in Latin. But a little later he was seen to accept the book 'and read it before her grace'. It is supposed that with the book the Queen had sent a message that Oglethorpe should read the Gospel and Epistle in English as well as Latin. Be that as it may, he did so; and a breach was for the first time made in the exclusive Latinity of the service.

Elizabeth does not appear to have been impressed by the ceremony of Anointing for, according to Gabriel Goodman, later Dean of Westminster, when she retired behind her traverse to change her robes she remarked to her maids 'that the oil was grease and smelled ill'. The service over, the Queen processed to Westminster Hall for the traditional banquet. The same Sir Edward Dymoke, who had been the Champion of England at Queen Mary's coronation, again performed his ceremonial task of casting down his gauntlet as a challenge to fight anyone who denied that Elizabeth was 'lawful queen of this realm'.

There was a change in the style and titles of the Queen as proclaimed by Garter King of Arms:

> . . . the most high and mighty princess, our dread sovereign, lady Elizabeth, by the grace of God, queen of England, France, Ireland, Defender of the true, ancient, and catholic faith, most worthy empress from the Orcade Isles to the Mountains Pyrenée. A Largess, a largess, a largess.

It seems plain that Elizabeth was not yet ready to proclaim herself

Head of the Church, but the curious phrase 'most worthy empress from the Orcade Isles to the Mountains Pyrenée' would seem to imply that she was indicating that she would take under her wing all who were currently renouncing the authority of the Pope, from the Calvinists in the North of Scotland to the reformers in the South of France.

Elizabeth was, however, still playing her hand cautiously. Although she sent private assurances to the Kings of Denmark and Sweden and to the Protestant Princes of Germany of her attachment to the reformed faith, she instructed the English Minister in Rome to announce her accession to the aged Pope Paul IV and assure him 'that it was not her intention to offer violence to the consciences of any denomination of her subjects, on the score of religion'. The Pope replied 'that he was unable to comprehend the hereditary right of one not born in wedlock, that the queen of Scots claimed the crown, as the nearest legitimate descendant of Henry VII, but that if Elizabeth were willing to submit the controversy to his arbitration, every indulgence should be shewn to her which justice would permit.' Upon this Elizabeth recalled the representative whom her sister had maintained in Rome. On 12 January 1559 the Pope issued a Bull 'declaring heretical sovereigns incapable of reigning'. However, Elizabeth was not mentioned by name and all the Catholic peers paid homage to her at her coronation. The Pope was no more anxious for an immediate breach than was the Queen.

CHAPTER 9

QUEEN MARY II

The coronation of the third Sovereign Queen, Mary II, was notable for being the only coronation of joint Sovereigns in English history. James II had fled and, by the 'Glorious Whig Revolution' of 1688, Parliament had bestowed the crown jointly upon his daughter Mary and her husband William, Prince of Orange. A duplicate set of Regalia had to be made for the occasion.

William and Mary walked through the Abbey side by side as joint Sovereigns with the Sword of State between them. The Queen's sister, Princess Anne, who was not on good terms with the Queen, but was standing by the throne, half graciously, half disdainfully remarked, 'Madam, I pity your fatigue'. The Queen tartly replied, 'A crown, sister, is not so heavy as it seems'. Archbishop Sancroft absented himself and the ceremony was performed by Bishop Compton of London.

The diarist Evelyn noted:

> I saw the Procession to and from the Abby Church of Westminster, with the great feaste in Westminster Hall, at the Coronation of King William and Queen Mary. What was different from former Coronations was some alteration in the Coronation oath. Dr Burnet, now made Bishop of Sarum, preach'd with greate applause. The Parliament men had scaffolds and places which took up one whole side of the Hall. When the King and Queen had dined, the ceremonie of the Champion, and other services by tenure were perform'd. The Parliament men were feasted in the Exchequer Chamber, and had each of them a (Coronation) gold medal given them, worth five and forty shillings. On one side were the effigies of the King and Queene inclining one to the other; on the reverse was Jupiter throwing a bolt at Phaeton, the words 'Ne totus absumater'; which was but dull, seeing that they might have had out of the poet something as apposite.
>
> Much of the splendour of the proceeding was abated by the absence of divers who should have contributed to it, there being but five Bishops, foure Judges (no more being yet sworn), and severall noblemen, and great ladys wanting; the feast, however, was magnificent. The next day the House of Commons went and kiss'd their new Majestie's hands in the Banquetting House.

Until this coronation the canopy held by the four Knights of the Garter had been used to shield the Sovereign from the public gaze while being anointed. William and Mary were anxious that the Parliament to whom they owed their crowns should see this part of the ceremony; they therefore stood up and faced the stand containing the members of the House of Commons. It was at this coronation, too, that the presentation of the Bible was first introduced into the Service.

King James had fled the realm on 11 December 1688. The Prince of Orange and his Dutch and English troops had meanwhile reached Windsor. Mary landed from Holland on 12 February 1689. The unnatural joy which she showed on entering into her father's inheritance and property was adversely commented on alike by the Jacobites and by the adherents of the House of Orange. Evelyn wrote:

> She came into Whitehall, jolly as to a wedding, seeming quite transported with joy.

Sarah Jennings, Lady Churchill, soon to become Countess Marlborough and in the next reign Duchess of Marlborough, etched the new Queen's conduct with her most searing acids:

> Queen Mary wanted bowels [of compassion]; of this she gave unquestionable proof the first day she came to Whitehall. She ran about it looking into every closet and conveniencey, and turning up the quilts of the beds just as people do at an inn, with no sort of concern in her appearance. Although at the time I was extremely caressed by her, I thought this strange and unbecoming conduct. For whatever necessity there was of deposing king James, he was still her father, who had been lately driven from that very chamber, and from that bed; and, if she felt no tenderness, I thought, at least, she might have felt grave, or even pensively sad, at so melancholy a reverse of fortune. But I kept these thoughts in my own breast, not even imparting them to my mistress, the princess Anne, to whom I could say anything.

The new Sovereigns were proclaimed on Ash Wednesday, the first day of Lent. The coronation took place on April 11. While the King and Queen were robing themselves for the coronation the news arrived that James had landed at Kinsale in Ireland and that he had secured the whole of the island with the exception of Londonderry and a few other towns. Almost at the same time the Lord Chamberlain, Lord Nottingham, handed to the Queen the first letter her father James II had written to her since her accession. The letter said:

> That hitherto he had made all fatherly excuses of what had been done, and had wholly attributed her part in the revolution to obedience to her husband, but the act of being crowned was in her own power, and if she were crowned while he and the prince of Wales were living,

the curses of an outraged father would light upon her, as well as of that God who had commanded duty to parents.

The bad news from Ireland coupled with the justly reproachful letter from James threw the King and Queen into an altercation which delayed their coronation. A contemporary chronicler records that:

'All was ready for the coronation at eleven o'clock', but 'the ceremony did not commence till half-past one'. William had been rowed in his royal barge from Whitehall to the Palace of Westminster nearly an hour ahead of the Queen. She followed him in a chair, wearing her Parliamentary robes and a circlet of gold richly adorned with precious stones. On arrival at Westminster, the Queen's train was borne by the Duchess of Somerset, her aunt Lady Henrietta Hyde, Lady Diana Vere, Lady Elizabeth Cavendish and Lady Elizabeth Paulet.

Under these difficult circumstances the coronation passed off with only minor hitches, such as that when the King and Queen were kneeling at the altar and should have made their first offering the King found that the envelope which should have contained twenty guineas was empty. The Queen had no money either and a long pause ensued, 'which everyone began to deem excessively ridiculous' until Lord Danby drew out his purse and placed twenty guineas in the gold basin on the King's behalf.

A large pearl and several pieces of plate 'bearing the royal arms were lost or stolen at the coronation' and 'a notice had to be placed in the Gazette, inviting those who had them to return them to the board of green-cloth'. History does not relate whether there was any answer to this appeal.

Soon after their coronation William and Mary assumed the sovereignty of Scotland in London. Their commissioners were unable to take possession of the Scottish Regalia which was securely held by the Duke of Gordon for Mary's father, James II, in Edinburgh Castle. However, a number of Scottish peers and notabilities headed by the Earl of Argyle assembled in the banqueting house in Whitehall and assured the King and Queen that they had been called to the Scottish throne by the unanimous vote of the Senate. Dundee and others were already in arms at the time.

Argyle recited the Scottish coronation oath and William and Mary repeated it after him word by word, holding up their right hands according to the Scottish custom. When Argyle reached the words 'and we shall be careful to root out all heretics' William interrupted and said, 'If this means any sort of persecution, I will not take the oath'. Argyle replied, 'It was not meant in any such sense' and he resumed:

> And we shall be careful to root out all heretics, and enemies to the true worship of God, that shall be convicted, by the true kirk of God, of the aforesaid crimes, out of our lands and empire of Scotland. And we faithfully affirm the things above written by our solemn oath.

Before the King and Queen put their signatures to the oath, Argyle explained that 'obstinate heretics by the law of Scotland can only be outlawed and their moveable goods confiscated'. William and Mary, it seems, did not regard such action as tantamount to persecution and signed without more ado. But we who live in the age of the gas-chamber are scarcely in a position to make mock of the relative tolerance and liberalism of our forebears.

CHAPTER 10

QUEEN ANNE

Queen Anne succeeded to the throne at the age of thirty-seven on the death of her brother-in-law, William III, on 8 March 1702. Her sister, Mary, who had reigned jointly with William had died eight years before him. The King had been long adying in Kensington Palace following upon a riding accident he had sustained at Hampton Court when his horse, Sorrell, stumbled and he fell against the pommell. News of his condition was anxiously awaited by the Princess Anne and her friend, Lady Marlborough, at St James's Palace. Throughout Saturday night and Sunday morning of March 8 King William's Lord Chamberlain, Lord Jersey, sent a series of hurried notes describing 'how the breath of William III grew shorter and shorter'. Anne had organised her own intelligence service, but it is a sad commentary upon human nature to have to record that there was much competition to be the first at St James's Palace with the good news of the King's death. Lord Dartmouth recorded at the time:

> As soon as the breath was out of king William, by which event all expectations from him were for ever at an end, off set Dr Burnet, bishop of Salisbury, and drove hard to bring the first tidings of the king's demise to St. James's Palace, where he prostrated himself at the new queen's feet, full of joy and duty; but he obtained no advantage over the earl of Essex (the lord of the bedchamber, then in waiting, whose proper office it was to communicate the event), besides being universally laughed at for his officiousness.

This story is confirmed by the spy, Mackey, who wrote: 'On the queen's accession to the throne, the bishop was the first that brought her the news of king William's death; yet he was turned out of his lodgings at court, and met with several affronts.'

Many of the new Queen's subjects were still Jacobites at heart and had scruples about taking the oath of allegiance. Among those who crowded in upon the Queen's apartments on that Sunday morning was her uncle, the Earl of Clarendon. He desired of the Lord in Waiting 'admittance to his niece'; but the Queen sent word to him 'that if he would go and qualify himself to enter her presence, she would be very glad to see him'. The Lord in Waiting expanded this Delphic utterance by asking whether he was willing to take the oath of allegiance to Queen Anne. 'No,' replied Clarendon; 'I come to talk to my niece; I shall take no other oaths than I have taken.' 'And,' smugly wrote Roger Coke, a contemporary pamphleteer, 'that wretched man remained a non-juror to the day of his death'.

Although it was a Sunday, both Houses of Parliament met that morning and Loyal Addresses were carried and presented to the Queen the same evening. Anne received the deputations and replied to them herself in the exceptionally beautiful voice for which she was renowned. Her Uncle, Charles II, had liked it so well that he had entrusted Mrs Betterton, the famous actress, with the task of giving the young Princess Anne elocution lessons.

Scotland at this time was still a separate kingdom. On March 13 the Scottish Council was summoned and Anne was proclaimed Queen of Scotland by Lord Lyon King of Arms. While St James's Palace was being draped in black mourning, the Queen retired to Windsor. She fixed her coronation for only six weeks later, St George's Day April 23, the anniversary of the coronation of her father, James II, and of that of her uncle Charles II. She announced at the same time that deep mourning was to cease after the coronation. 'The Postman' of 19 March 1702 recorded an early 'Buy British' campaign:

> For the encouragement of our English silks, called a-la-modes, his royal highness, the prince of Denmark, and the nobility, appear in mourning hat-bands made of that silk, to bring the same in fashion in the place of crape, which are made in the pope's country, whither we send our money for them.

The House of Commons voted the Queen the same revenue as had been granted 'to king William, of blessed memory'; and the Queen went to the House of Lords on March 30 to give her assent to the Bills which had been carried. She told the Commons:

> I will straiten myself in my own expenses, rather than not contribute all I can to my subjects' ease and relief. It is probable the revenue may fall short of what it has formerly produced; however, I will give directions that £100,000 be applied to the public service in this year out of the revenue you have so unanimously given me.

The Queen and her husband, Prince George of Denmark, excited some adverse comment by the speed with which they took possession of Kensington Palace and the inadequacy of the ceremonial at the funeral of the late King, which took place at midnight. Bishop Burnet, though a strong critic of William, feeling himself no doubt to have been rebuffed by Anne commented ''Twas scarce decent.'

The Jacobite Party had no intention of wearing mourning for William III, but, like Queen Anne, they were already in mourning for James II who had died the year before. A Jacobite poet gave vent to these contrary emotions in a broadside which was widely distributed during the weeks between King William's funeral and Queen Anne's coronation:

> In sable weeds your beaux and belles appear,
> And cloud the coming beauties of the year.
> Mourn on, ye foolish fashionable things,
> Mourn for your own misfortunes, not the king's:
> Mourn for the mighty mass of coin misspent –
> Most prodigally given, and idly spent.
> Mourn for your tapestry, and your statues too,
> Our Windsor gutted to adorn his Loo.
> Mourn for the mitre long from Scotland gone,
> And much more mourn your union coming on.
> Mourn for a ten years' war and dismal weather,
> And taxes strung like necklaces together,
> On salt, malt, paper, cyder, lights, and leather.
> Much for the civil list need not be said,
> They truly mourn who are fifteen months unpaid.
> Well, then, my friends, since things you see are so,
> Let's e'en mourn on; 'twould lessen much our wo,
> Had Sorrel stumbled thirteen years ago!
> Your sea has oft run purple to the shore,
> And Flanders been manured with English gore.

At the time of her coronation Queen Anne was suffering from a severe attack of gout. She was only just thirty-seven, but the combination of gout and the bearing of children had sapped her health. Five years later she had buried sixteen; none survived her. She was certainly the only infirm person who was ever crowned King or Queen of England. Gouty and corpulent, she had lost the use of her feet and had to be carried to Westminster Hall in a sedan chair at about 11 o'clock in the morning. After she had been enthroned in Westminster Hall, and the Regalia had been distributed, the procession was marshalled. This was the first and last time, till the coronation of Queen Elizabeth II, that a Sovereign Queen had had a husband at the time of her coronation. The Queen's husband, Prince George of Denmark, had been naturalised and created Duke of Cumberland, with precedence before all other Peers, at the coronation of William and Mary. No question was, however, entertained of his mounting the throne with Anne as

William had done with Mary. The order of the procession is of particular interest since it will be followed in many particulars in 1953, two hundred and fifty-one years later. It is set out below:—

PLAN OF THE PROCESSION

Lord Privy Seal   Lord Archbishop of York
Lord Keeper of the Great Seal   Lord Archbishop of
with the purse   Canterbury

Two Persons to Represent the Dukes of Aquitaine and Normandy in Crimson Velvet Mantles, lined with Meniver, powdered with Ermine, each of them his cap in his Hand, of Cloth of Gold, furr'd and powdered with Ermine

His Royal Highness *Prince George of Denmark*,
his Train borne by his Master of the Robes

St. Edward's Staff, borne by the Earl of Dorset	The Scepter, with the Cross, by the E. of Huntingdon	The Golden Spurs, by the Ld. Vis. Longueville
The Third Sword, by the E. of Pembroke, Lord High Admiral of England	Curtana, by the Earl of Kent	The Pointed Sword, by the Earl of Derby
The Lord Mayor of London, bearing the City Mace, in a Gown of Crimson Velvet, wearing His Collar and Jewel	Garter, Principal King of Arms, wearing his Collar and Jewel, his Coronet in his Hand	The Gentleman Usher of the Black Rod, with the Black Rod in his Hand

The Lord Great Chamberlain in his Robes,
with his Coronet and White Staff in his Hand

Serjeants at Arms

The Earl Marshal of England in his Robes, with his Coronet in his Hand, and Earl Marshal's Staff	The Sword of State in the Scabard, borne by the Earl of Oxford	The Lord High Constable of England in his Robes, with his Staff and Coronet in his Hand; the Duke of Bedford
The Queen's Scepter, with the Dove, borne by the Duke of Richmond	The Crown, borne by the Duke of Devonshire, Lord High Steward	The Orbe, borne by the Duke of Somerset, Lord President of the Council
The Paten, by the Ld. Bishop of Sarum	The Bible, by the Lord Bishop of Worcester	The Chalice, by the Ld. Bishop of Rochester

Serjeants at Arms

The Canopy, born by 16 Barons of the Cinque-Ports, *over the*

QUEEN

Gentlemen Pensioners

Supporter, the Lord Bishop of Exeter[1]	THE QUEEN, in Her Royal Robes of Crimson Velvet, Furr'd with Ermine, and Border'd with Gold Lace; on her Head a Circlet of Gold, wearing the Great Collar and George: Her Train borne by a Duchess in her Robes, assisted by four Ladies and the Queen's Lord Chamberlain	Supporter, the Lord Bishop of Durham

Gentlemen Pensioners

[1] The Bishop of Exeter was called upon to be one of the Queen's supporters since the Bishop of Bath and Wells declined to attend, being in his heart a dissenter.

It will be noted that, next to the Queen and the Regalia (from which the Sovereign cannot be separated) Prince George had the most honourable position in the procession, outranking not only Great Officers of the Realm such as the Lord Privy Seal and the Lord Keeper of the Great Seal (the Lord Chancellor), but even the two Archbishops. Queen Anne's coronation is of interest as being the last occasion when two gentlemen played the roles of the Dukes of Normandy and Aquitaine. This was an obsolete survival from the times when the Kings of England ruled over large areas of France. The two gentlemen of the privy chamber who discharged these tasks bore more modest names in real life than those they represented at the coronation – James Clark and Jonathan Andrews.

The Queen was carried in her 'open chair' from Westminster Hall to the Abbey. It is not clear from contemporary accounts whether she was carried in the Abbey itself, but her two supporting Bishops were undoubtedly called upon for more than a merely token or spiritual discharge of their duties. Not only did they have to support the heavy crown but, when she was standing, the Queen herself. The Queen's train was borne by the Duchess of Somerset assisted by four Ladies of the Bedchamber and the Lord Chamberlain. The service was conducted by Tenison, Archbishop of Canterbury.

Despite her infirmity, Queen Anne discharged her first offertory with greater success than her immediate predecessors, William and Mary, who, when the exhortation was read 'Thou shalt not appear before the Lord thy God empty' found themselves embarrassed by having omitted to provide themselves with a suitable offering. Anne put the necessary donative 'in the gold basons' and then made all her oblations as required.

The Queen had to make the same protestant declaration as had been made by William and Mary. Despite her illness, she did not dispense with the ceremony of standing to be girt with the Sword of St Edward and thereafter she carried it herself and offered it at the altar. The peer who redeemed it and carried it from then on naked before the Queen was the last of a famous family, Aubrey de Vere, 20th Earl of Oxford. He had borne the Sword Curtana at the coronation of Charles II and the Sword of State at that of James II and William and Mary – a record of service at four successive coronations which has only been surpassed by Thomas, 8th Earl of Pembroke, who carried the 2nd or 3rd Swords at the coronations of James II, William and Mary and Anne; and the Sword Curtana at those of George I and George II.

The Queen set the precedent for subsequent Sovereign Queens by not having the Spurs momentarily set on her heels; she merely touched them and sent them directly back to the altar. Like her sister, Mary II, she did not have the Coronation Ring of Edward the Confessor placed upon her finger. Her father, James II, had taken it with him into exile and it was not until some generations later that his last surviving grandson, Cardinal York, returned it to the Royal Family. Instead she wore a ring with a balas or spinel ruby of a delicate shade of rose pink.

After the crowning, Prince George, as Duke of Cumberland and the senior peer, did homage before the Archbishops and Bishops. Though by Act of Parliament he had been granted precedence of the Archbishop this has been thought unseemly, and the precedent is unlikely to be followed by the Duke of Edinburgh, although outside Parliament his precedence is second only to that of the Queen. The prayer for the Royal Family, strangely enough, omitted Prince George and merely ended with the supplication '. . . bless Catherine the queen-dowager, and the whole royal family'. It was strange that this childless Roman Catholic widow of Charles II was the only person besides the Sovereign prayed for by name in the prayers of the Church of England. Catherine of Braganza, who was then a woman of sixty-four, was living in Portugal and two years later was to become Queen Regent of that country on behalf of her brother, Pedro.

In her ill-state of health Queen Anne might well have been inclined to dispense with the traditional banquet in Westminster Hall, but if she had done so her Jacobite subjects might have proffered the jibe that she did not dare run the risk that the challenge of her Champion Sir Edward Dymoke might be accepted. All went off well and nothing occurred to mar the ceremonies.

It was 8.30 in the evening before the Queen could be carried back in her 'close sedan chair' to St James's Palace. Prince George of Denmark seemed disposed to pass the evening carousing with his friends and drinking the Queen's health. The Lord Chamberlain noticed how tired the Queen was and suggested to the Duke that he should propose going to bed. '*I* propose,' replied the Prince jovially, '*I* cannot, I am her majesty's subject – have done and sworn homage to her to-day; I shall do nought but what she commands me.' 'Then,' replied Queen Anne, laughing, 'as that is the case, as I am very tired, I do command you, George, to come to bed.' In this decorous and conjugal fashion Queen Anne's coronation day came to an end.

CHAPTER 11

QUEEN VICTORIA

Queen Victoria, the fifth Sovereign Queen of England and the thirty-fifth Sovereign in succession from William the Conqueror is the only monarch who has left a detailed record of her coronation day. When one considers that the Queen was only nineteen, that she had been awake since 4 o'clock in the morning and that she did not sit down to write her journal until nearly midnight, one cannot but admire the vitality and self-discipline which were to sustain her during the sixty-four years of her reign and which must be accounted the most glorious and happy period the British people have ever known.

Thursday, 28th June 1838.

I was awoke at four o'clock by the guns in the Park, and could not get much sleep afterwards on account of the noise of the people, bands, etc., etc. Got up at seven, feeling strong and well; the Park presented a curious spectacle, crowds of people up to Constitution Hill, soldiers, bands, etc. I dressed, having taken a little breakfast before I dressed, and a little after. At half past 9 I went into the next room, dressed exactly in my House of Lords costume; and met Uncle Ernest, Charles and Feodore (who had come a few minutes before into my dressing room), Lady Lansdowne, Lady Normanby, the Duchess of Sutherland, and Lady Barham, all in their robes.

At 10 I got into the State Coach with the Duchess of Sutherland and Lord Albemarle and we began our Progress. I subjoin a minute account of the whole Procession and of the whole Proceeding – the route, etc. It was a fine day, and the crowds of people exceeded what I have ever seen; many as there were the day I went to the City, it was nothing, nothing to the multitudes, the millions of my loyal subjects who were assembled *in every spot* to witness the Procession. Their good humour and excessive loyalty was beyond everything, and I really cannot say *how* proud I feel to be the Queen of *such* a Nation. I was alarmed at times for fear that the people would be crushed and squeezed on account of the tremendous rush and pressure.

I reached the Abbey amid deafening cheers at a little after half past eleven; I first went into a robing room quite close to the entrance where I found my eight train-bearers; Lady Caroline Lennox, Lady Adelaide Paget, Lady Mary Talbot, Lady Fanny Cowper, Lady Wilhelmina Stanhope, Lady Anne Fitz-william, Lady Mary Grimston, and Lady

Queen Elizabeth's River Procession from Westminster to the Tower on
the eve of her Coronation

The gent pencionars on foote withe pollares In their handes bareheaded

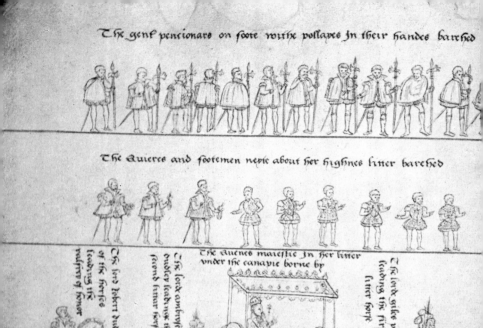

The Quieres and footemen nere about her highnes litter bareheaded

The Quenes maiestie In her litter
vnder the canapie borne by

The lord gilles pawlet
leading the firste
litter horse

The lord amprose
dudley leadinge the
second litter horse

The lord Robert dudley mr
of the horsse
leading the
palfrey of honor

The Quieres and footemen nere aboute her highnes litter bareheaded

The gent pencionars on foote withe pollares In their handes bareheaded

Louisa Jenkinson – all dressed alike and beautifully in white satin and silver tissue with wreaths of silver corn-ears in front, and a small one of pink roses round the plait behind, and pink roses in the trimming of the dresses.

After putting on my mantle, and the young ladies having properly got hold of it and Lord Conyngham holding the end of it, I left the robing-room and the Procession began as is described in the annexed account, and all that followed and took place. The sight was splendid; the bank of Peeresses quite beautiful all in their robes, and the Peers on the other side. My young train-bearers were always near me, and helped me whenever I wanted anything. The Bishop of Durham stood on the side near me, but he was, as Lord Melbourne told me, remarkably maladroit, and never could tell me what was to take place. At the beginning of the Anthem, where I've made a mark, I retired to St Edward's Chapel, a dark small place immediately behind the Altar, with my ladies and train-bearers – took off my crimson robe and kirtle, and put on the supertunica of cloth of gold, also in the shape of the kirtle, which was put over a singular sort of little gown of linen trimmed with lace; I also took off my circlet of diamonds and then proceeded bare-headed into the Abbey; I was then seated upon St Edward's chair, where the Dalmatic robe was clasped round me by the Lord Great Chamberlain. Then followed all the various things; and last (of those things) the Crown being placed on my head – which was, I must own, a most beautiful impressive moment; *all* the Peers and Peeresses put on their coronets at the same instant.

My excellent Lord Melbourne who stood very close to me throughout the whole ceremony, was *completely* overcome at this moment, and very much affected; he gave me *such* a kind, and I may say *fatherly* look. The shouts, which were very great, the drums, the trumpets, the firing of the guns, all at the same instant, rendered the spectacle most imposing.

This illustration, for permission to publish which I am indebted to the College of Arms, is thought by some to be the oldest surviving contemporary drawing of an English coronation. This and other drawings of great personages in the procession were drawn by a herald. He apparently made rough pen and ink sketches (which still exist in the British Museum) on the spot and from them later made more detailed drawings
The fact that the Queen is portrayed wearing her crown and carrying her sceptre makes it unlikely that these drawings depict the actual coronation procession from the Tower since the Regalia would have been awaiting her in the Abbey and there would hardly have been any question of a mounted procession after the ceremony merely to Westminster Hall. It seems more probable that what is portrayed was the Royal procession ten days later when the Queen, in her Parliamentary robes, went with all the peers spiritual and temporal to Westminster Abbey for a religious service

The Enthronisation and the Homage of, first, all the Bishops, and then my Uncles, and lastly of all the Peers, in their respective order was very fine. The Duke of Norfolk (holding for me the Sceptre with a Cross) with Lord Melbourne stood close to me on my right, and the Duke of Richmond with the other Sceptre behind the Throne. Poor old Lord Rolle, who is 82, and dreadfully infirm, in attempting to ascend the steps fell and rolled quite down, but was not the least hurt; when he attempted to re-ascend them I got up and advanced to the end of the steps, in order to prevent another fall. When Lord Melbourne's turn to do Homage came, there was loud cheering; they also cheered Lord Grey and the Duke of Wellington; it's a pretty ceremony; they first all touch the Crown, and then kiss my hand. When my good Lord Melbourne knelt down and kissed my hand, he pressed my hand and I grasped his with all my heart, at which he looked up with his eyes filled with tears and seemed much touched, as he was, I observed, throughout the whole ceremony. After the Homage was concluded I left the Throne, took off my Crown and received the Sacrament; I then put on my Crown again, and re-ascended the Throne, leaning on Lord Melbourne's arm. At the commencement of the Anthem I descended from the Throne, and went into St Edward's Chapel with my Ladies, Train-bearers, and Lord Willoughby, where I took off the Dalmatic robe, supertunica, etc., and put on the Purple Velvet Kirtle and Mantle, and proceeded again to the Throne, which I ascended leaning on Lord Melbourne's hand.

There was another most dear Being present at this ceremony, in the box immediately above the royal box, and who witnessed all; it was my dearly beloved angelic Lehzen, whose eyes I caught when on the Throne, and we exchanged smiles. She and Späth, Lady John Russell, and Mr Murray saw me leave the Palace, arrive at the Abbey, leave the Abbey and again return to the Palace!!

I then again descended from the Throne, and repaired with all the Peers bearing the Regalia, my Ladies and Train-bearers, to St Edward's Chapel, as it is called; but which, as Lord Melbourne said, was more *un*like a Chapel than anything he had ever seen; for what was *called* an *Altar* was covered with sandwiches, bottles of wine, etc, etc. The Archbishop came in and *ought* to have delivered the Orb to me, but I had already got it, and he (as usual) was *so* confused and puzzled and knew nothing, and – went away. Here we waited some minutes. Lord Melbourne took a glass of wine, for he seemed completely tired. The Procession being formed, I replaced my Crown (which I had taken off for a few minutes), took the Orb in my left hand and the Sceptre in my right, and thus loaded, proceeded through the Abbey – which resounded with cheers, to the first robing room; where I found the Duchess of Gloucester, Mamma, and the Duchess of Cambridge with their Ladies. And here we waited for at least an hour, with *all* my ladies and train-bearers; the Princesses went away about half an hour before I did. The Archbishop had (most awkwardly) put the ring on the wrong finger, and the consequence was that I had the greatest difficulty to take it off again, which I at last did with great pain. Lady Fanny, Lady Wilhelmina, and Lady Mary Grimston, looked quite beautiful. At about half past four I re-entered my carriage, the Crown on my head, and the Sceptre and Orb in my hands, and we proceeded the same way as we came – the crowds if possible having increased. The enthusiasm, affection, and loyalty were really touching, and I shall ever remember this day as the *Proudest* of my life! I came home at a little after six, really *not* feeling tired.

At eight we dined. Besides we thirteen – my Uncles, sister, brother, Späth, and the Duke's gentlemen – my excellent Lord Melbourne and Lord Surrey dined here. Lord Melbourne came up to me and said: 'I must congratulate you on this most brilliant day', and that all had gone off so well. He said he was not tired, and was in high spirits. I sat between Uncle Ernest[1] and Lord Melbourne; and Lord Melbourne between me and Feodore, whom he had led in. My kind Lord Melbourne was much affected in speaking of the whole ceremony. He asked kindly if I was tired; said the Sword he carried (the first, the Sword of State) was excessively heavy. I said that the Crown hurt me a good deal. He was so much amused at Uncle Ernest's being astonished at our still having the Litany. We agreed that the whole thing was a very fine sight. He thought the robes, and particularly the Dalmatic, 'looked remarkably well'. 'And you did it all so well – excellent!' said he, with tears in his eyes. He said he thought I looked rather pale and 'moved by all the people' when I arrived; 'and that's natural; and that's better'. The Archbishop's and Dean's copes, which were remarkably handsome, were from James the Second's time; the very same that were worn at his Coronation, Lord Melbourne told me. Spoke of the Bishop of Durham's awkwardness, Lord Rolle's fall, etc. Of the Duc de Nemours being like his father in face; of the young ladies and he said he thought the Duchess of Richmond (who had ordered the make of the dresses, etc, and had been much condemned by some of the young ladies for it) quite right. She said to him: 'One thing I was determined about; that I would have no discussion with their Mammas about it.' Spoke of Talleyrand and Soult having been very much struck by the ceremony of the Coronation; of the English being far too generous *not* to be kind to Soult. Lord Melbourne went home the night before, and slept very deeply till he was woke at six in the morning. I said I did not sleep well. Spoke of the Illuminations and Uncle Ernest's wish to see them.

After dinner, before we sat down, we (that is Charles, Lord Melbourne, and I) spoke of the numbers of Peers at the Coronation, which, Lord Melbourne said, with the tears in his eyes, was unprecedented. I observed that there were very few Viscounts; he said: 'There are very few Viscounts', that they were an odd sort of title and not really English; that they came from Vice-Comites; that Dukes and Barons were the only *real* English titles; that Marquises were likewise not English; and

[1] The King of Hanover.

that they made people Marquises when they did not wish to make them Dukes. Spoke of Lord Audley who came as the First Baron, and who Lord Melbourne said was a very odd young man, but of a very old family; his ancestor was a Sir Something Audley in the time of the Black Prince, who, with Chandos, gained the Battle of Poictiers.

I then sat on the sofa for a little while with Lady Barham and then with Charles; Lord Melbourne sitting near me the whole evening. Mamma and Feodore remained to see the illuminations and only came in later, and Mamma went away before I did. Uncle Ernest drove out to see the illuminations.

I said to Lord Melbourne when I first sat down that I felt a little tired on my feet; 'You must be very tired,' he said. Spoke of the weight of the Robes, etc, etc, the Coronets; and he turned round to me with the tears in his eyes, and said *so* kindly: 'And you did it beautifully – every part of it, with so much taste; it's a thing that you can't give a person advice upon; it must be left to a person.' To hear this, from this kind impartial friend, gave me great and real pleasure. Mamma and Feodore came back just after he said this. Spoke of the Bishops' Copes, about which he was very funny; of the Pages who were such a nice set of boys, and who were so handy, Lord Melbourne said, that they kept them the whole time. Little Lord Stafford and Slane (Lord Mountcharles) were pages to their fathers and looked lovely; Lord Paget (not a fine boy) was Lord Melbourne's page and remarkably handy, he said. Spoke again of the young ladies' dresses, about which he was very amusing; he waited for his carriage with Lady Mary Talbot and Lady Wilhelmina; he thinks Lady Fanny does not make as much show as other girls, which I would not allow. He set off for the Abbey from his house at half past eight, and was there long before anybody else; he only got home at half past six and had to go round by Kensington. He said there was a large breakfast in the Jerusalem Chamber where they met *before* all began; he said, laughing, that whenever the Clergy, or a Dean and Chapter, had anything to do with anything, there's sure to be plenty to eat.

Spoke of my intending to go to bed, etc, he said, 'You may depend upon it, you are more tired than you think you are.' I said I had slept badly the night before; he said that was my mind, that nothing kept people more awake than any consciousness of a great event going to take place, and being agitated. He was not sure if he was not going to the Duke of Wellington's.

Stayed in the dining room till twenty minutes past eleven, but remained on Mamma's balcony looking at the fireworks in Green Park which was quite beautiful.

Uncle Ernest, Charles, Feodore, and the Ladies and Gentlemen (like Lehzen, etc) saw me leave the Palace, arrive at the Abbey, leave the Abbey, and return to the Palace. Got a long letter from Aunt Louise.

The Champion's Challenge at the Coronation of King James II

PART III

CHAPTER 12

THE MOST MAGNIFICENT OF CORONATIONS: THE CROWNING OF 'PRINNY'

The coronation of King George IV in 1821 was notable for a number of reasons. It was the most elaborate, costly and magnificent pageant ever staged by an English king. The costumes of all the leading participants were specially designed for the occasion and the King himself, who as Prince Regent had won the title of 'The First Gentleman in Europe', personally supervised every detail of dress and ceremonial.

It is of interest too because it was the last occasion on which two traditional ceremonies took place in Westminster Hall – the enthronement by the peers before the Abbey ceremony and the banquet which traditionally followed it. The occasion was memorable too for the fact that the King announced that he would not permit Queen Caroline either to be crowned with him or to attend the ceremony. On 7 May 1821 the Prime Minister, Lord Liverpool, had written to the Queen as follows:

'Lord Liverpool has received the King's commands, in consequence of the last communication of the Queen to Lord Liverpool of the 5th inst., to inform the Queen that his majesty having determined that the Queen shall form no part of the ceremonial of his coronation, it is therefore the royal pleasure that the Queen shall not attend the said ceremony.'

However, she set out at five o'clock in the morning from her house in Mayfair in a coach drawn by six bays. Having vainly sought admittance to Westminster Hall by three separate doors, she went on foot to the House of Lords where she was also refused entry.

Finally she drove to the Abbey where, according to Dean Stanley, 'Sir Robert Inglis, then a young man, was charged with the duty of keeping order at that point. He heard a cry that the Queen was coming. He flew, rather than ran, to the door of the South Transept. She was leaning on Lord Hood's arm. He had but a moment to make up his mind how to meet her. "It is my duty", he said, "to announce to your Majesty that there is no place in the Abbey prepared for your Majesty." The Queen paused, and replied, "Am I to understand that you prevent me from entering the Abbey?" "Madam", he answered, in the same words, "it is my duty to announce to you that there is no place provided for your Majesty in the Abbey." She turned without a word. This was the final repulse. She who had come with deafening cheers retired in dead silence.' She got into her carriage once more and was driven away. A few weeks later she was dead.

There was immense competition to be present at this wonderful pageant and huge sums were paid for seats on the route. A dispute arose between the Lord Great Chamberlain and other high functionaries as to who was entitled to dispose of seats in Westminster Hall. The Dean and Chapter of Westminster farmed out the side aisle of the Abbey to a speculator, who fitted it up with boxes, which he let at a great profit. Every peer, instead of having to ballot as they did this year, was given 5 tickets, and the Lord Great Chamberlain was allotted 3,000 and the Lord High Steward 4,000.

Sir Walter Scott, who was present in the Abbey, commented thus:

'You must have heard a full account of the only disagreeable event of the day. I mean the attempt of the misguided Lady, who has lately furnished so many topics of discussion, to intrude herself upon a ceremonial, where, not being in her proper place, to be present in any other must have been voluntary degradation. The matter is a fire of straw, which has burned to the very embers; and those who try to blow it into life again, will only blacken their hands and noses, like mischievous children dabbling among the ashes of a bonfire.'

Perhaps the strangest aspect of this extraordinary ceremony is that more than half its cost was defrayed by France. Parliament had only voted £100,000 for the coronation; so the Government appropriated £138,238 0s 2d 'out of Money received from France on Account of pecuniary Indemnity, under Treaty, Anno 1815'.

Among the more expensive items in the bill was one of £8,205 15s 'for Snuff Boxes for Foreign Ministers' and £25,184 9s 8d for the expenses of the banquet which was organised by the Lord Steward, the Marquess of Cholmondeley. The banquet, as might have been expected from this vast expenditure, was of great splendour and all the old traditions were observed. The King was so pleased with the appearance of the Duke of Wellington as Lord High Constable, Lord Howard of Effingham as Deputy Earl Marshal, and the Marquess of Anglesey as Lord High Steward, who rode up the Hall at the head of the procession of servants bearing the dishes of the first course, that he invited them to dismount, and come to his chair and drink wine from a golden cup. The two former complied; Lord Anglesey, who had lost a leg at Waterloo where he commanded the British Cavalry, remained on his horse and, in reply to the King's remonstrance, pleaded that he could not walk as he had on his *riding* leg and could not send home for his *walking* leg.

After the first course Sir Edward Dymoke, the hereditary King's Champion, arrived on horseback in full armour with the Duke of Wellington on one side and Lord Howard of Effingham on the other. This was the last occasion on which this splendid medieval ceremony was performed.

It was a very hot day and the King had suffered greatly in the Abbey through the enormous weight and thickness of the robes he chose to wear. During the service he retired behind the traverse in St Edward's Chapel and took off all his peacock's clothes and sought to cool himself.

At the banquet in Westminster Hall the two thousand wax candles added appreciably to the heat. 'The very great heat', wrote one observer, 'was nowhere more visible than in the havoc which it made upon the curls of many of the ladies, several of whose heads had lost all traces of the friseur's skill long before the ceremony of the day had concluded'. The wax candles, too, melted and great drops fell 'without distinctions of persons' upon all within reach. The superb dresses of many of the peers and peeresses were spoiled by it, and escape was impossible 'for the wretched tenants of a slave ship were never more closely packed together. If a lovely female dared to raise her look to discover from what quarter the unwelcome visitation came, she was certain of receiving an additional patch upon her cheeks, which in order to disencumber herself of, obliged her to wipe away also the roseate hue which had been imparted to her countenance at her toilette, thereby obliging her to wear a double face, of nature on the one side, and of art on the other.'

While the banquet was proceeding, a hostile crowd gathered on the return route and the King was warned that it would be dangerous for him to return to Carlton House by the advertised route. He was advised to make a circuitous detour through Tothill Fields and the purlieus of Chelsea. One of the officers of the escort, Lord de Ros, who had been educated at Westminster and was familiar with the district, offered to act as guide along roads which were for the most part little better than country lanes. All sorts of obstacles were encountered en route and a bridge which had been condemned many years before as unsafe had to be crossed. Throughout the drive the King 'was horribly nervous, and kept continually calling to the officers of the escort to keep well up to the carriage windows'. After the strenuous glories of the day, King George's homecoming to Carlton House was a sad anti-climax.

THE CROWNING OF 'PRINNY'

On the following seven pages are reproduced coloured plates illustrating the occasion. The following is the key to them:—

PLATE (I)

King George IV is here seen leaving Carlton House in his State Coach the day before his Coronation to go to the Palace of Westminster where he spent the night in the Speaker's House.

PLATE (II)

King George IV sitting under the Cloth of Estate in Westminster Hall while the Dean of Westminster and six prebendaries deliver the regalia prior to them being handed by the Deputy Lord Great Chamberlain to the Noblemen and Bishops who are to carry them in the procession to the Abbey.

PLATE (III)

The King about to leave Westminster Hall for the Abbey. His train is borne by eight eldest sons of peers. The immense weight and thickness of his clothes caused the King much discomfort during the ceremony.

PLATE (IV)

The Archbishop placing the crown on the King's head. On the extreme left, carrying the Swords, are the Dukes of Newcastle and Northumberland; in the left foreground is the Duke of Devonshire; on the right is Prince Leopold of Saxe-Coburg-Gotha in the full habit of a Knight of the Garter; behind him is the Duke of Dorset carrying the jewelled Sword of State; in the right background is the Standard of England.

PLATE (V)

The scene in the Abbey as King George IV is crowned by the Archbishop of Canterbury.

PLATE (VI)

The King has been crowned and homage is now being paid by his brothers, the Royal Dukes of York, Clarence, Sussex, Cambridge and Gloucester.

PLATE (VII)

The King's Champion, Henry Dymoke, Esquire, arrives in Westminster Hall in armour to proclaim his challenge. On his left is the acting Earl Marshal, Lord Howard of Effingham (in place of the Duke of Norfolk who, as a Roman Catholic, was at that time barred from discharging his duties) and the Lord High Constable of England, the Duke of Wellington.

Plates (I), (II), (III), (V) and (VI) are reproduced from a contemporary book published in 1824 by Sir George Nayler, Garter King of Arms. Plates (IV) and (VII) are taken from a very rare book in the possession of the Duke of Buccleuch, to whom the author is indebted for permission to reproduce them here.

II

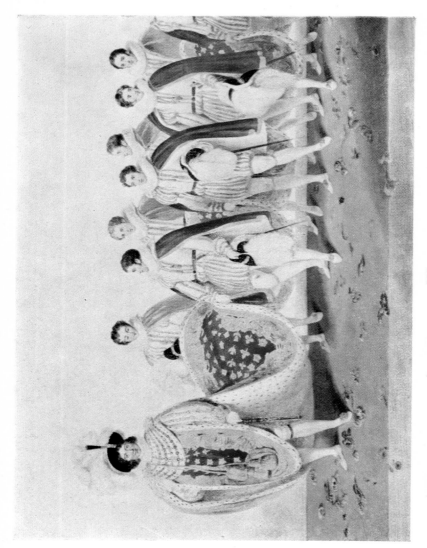

III

IV

V

VI

VII

PART IV

CHAPTER 13

THE CORONATION OATH

No part of the ceremony of crowning a modern constitutional monarch can be held to be of more importance than the Coronation Oath. It is only after the King or Queen has sworn on the Bible to govern according to law and custom; to administer justice with mercy; and to maintain the Protestant reformed religion and the rights and privileges of the bishops and clergy that the Archbishop anoints and crowns the Sovereign. The origins of the English Coronation Oath can be traced back through the oath administered to King Richard II in 1377 to Saxon times and may be ultimately rooted in a West Frankish Coronation Ordo in the year 900.

During the early Middle Ages the Coronation Oath was several times altered in form according to the fluctations in the relative bargaining powers of the King, the Church and the nobles. In the times when the monarchy was still partially elective, the Coronation Oath almost partook of the character of a parliamentary candidate's election address: the one who promised the most was the most likely to be crowned. Gradually order imposed itself upon this jungle of anarchy.

The Revolution of 1688, following upon the flight of James II, made possible the passage of the Bill of Rights of 1689 from whence stems the doctrine still valid to-day that 'Sovereignty resides in the King in his Parliament'. The Bill of Rights laid it down that

all and singular the rights and liberties asserted and claimed in the said Declaration [of Rights] are the true, auntient and indubitable rights and liberties of the people of this kingdome.

A Committee of the House of Commons also drafted an entirely new Coronation Oath which was embodied in an Act of Parliament (1 Will.&Mar.,cap.6) which started with the preamble:

foreasmuch as the oath . . . hath heretofore been framed in doubtful words and expressions with relation to antient laws and constitutions at this time unknown, to the end thereof that one uniform oath may be in all times to come taken by the Kings and Queens of this realm . . . may it please Your Majesties that it may be enacted . . .

In addition to the new Oath, the Act incorporated the famous Protestant declaration. This declaration, made by both William and Mary and by every sovereign from this time forward till the accession of King George V, was a condition precedent of being crowned and was as follows:

> I Mary, by the grace of God, queen of England, Scotland, France, and Ireland, Defender of the Faith, etc., do solemnly, in the presence of God, profess, testifie, and declare, that I do believe that in the sacrament of the Lord's Supper, there is not any transubstantiation of the elements of bread and wine into the body and blood of Christ, at or after the consecration thereof by any person whatsoever. 2ndly, That the invocation or adoration of the Virgin Mary, or any other saint, and the sacrifice of the mass, as they are now used in the church of Rome, are superstitious and idolatrous. 3rdly, And I do solemnly, in the presence of God, profess, testifie, and declare, that I do make this declaration, and every part thereof, in the plain and ordinary sense of the words read to me, as they are commonly understood by English Protestants, without any evasion, equivocation, or mental reservation whatsoever, and without any dispensation already granted me for this purpose by the Pope or any other authority or person, or without any hope of such dispensation from any person or authority whatsoever, or without thinking I am, or can be, acquitted before God or man, or absolved of this declaration, or of any part thereof, although the Pope, or any other person or power whatsoever, should dispense with, or annul the same, or declare that it was null and void from the beginning.

This flamboyant and illiberal declaration was deleted in 1910 at the express desire of King George V so as to avoid needless injury to his Roman Catholic subjects. Immediately upon coming to the throne, King George informed his Prime Minister, Mr Asquith, that he would not agree to open Parliament if he had to make the statutory declaration in this form. Mr Asquith sympathised with the King and submitted a revised declaration to the House of Commons. Numerous objections to the Asquith formula were received both from Nonconformists and from the Anglican Bishops. Ultimately the Archbishop of Canterbury proposed a new form of words, 'I declare I am a faithful Protestant and will uphold the Protestant succession'. This was incorporated in an Act of Parliament and has been used ever since.[1]

The late King George VI had not had a State opening of Parliament prior to his coronation and consequently had to sign the statutory declaration as well as the Oath in the Abbey. Queen Elizabeth II signed the declaration when she opened Parliament

[1] For a full account of this transaction see Sir Harold Nicolson's biography of King George V (pp. 162-3).

last November. Consequently on June 2 she will only have to swear and sign the Oath.

The evolutionary growth of the British Commonwealth and Empire has, over the last twenty years, necessitated changes in the styles and titles of the British Sovereign; and certain changes were introduced into the Oath in 1937. These were made necessary by the Statute of Westminster of 1936. Unfortunately, Mr Baldwin's Government which, under his leadership, was apt to be somewhat negligent in many matters both great and small, allowed themselves to be advised that as the changes were of a purely consequential character arising out of another Act of Parliament, there was no need to amend the Coronation Oath Act of 1689 which had been confirmed and applied to the United Kingdom of Great Britain by the Act of Union in 1707. Below are set out the two forms as used in 1911 and in 1937:—

1911	1937
Archbishop: Sir, is your Majesty willing to take the Oath?	*Archbishop:* Sir, is your Majesty willing to take the Oath?
King: I am willing.	*King:* I am willing.
Archbishop: Will you solemnly promise and swear to govern the people of this United Kingdom of Great Britain and Ireland, and the Dominions thereto belonging, according *to the Statutes in Parliament agreed on,* and the respective Laws and Customs of the same?	*Archbishop:* Will you solemnly promise and swear to govern *the peoples of Great Britain, Ireland, Canada, Australia, New Zealand and the Union of South Africa, of your Possessions and the other Territories to any of them belonging or pertaining, and of your Empire of India,* according to their respective laws and customs?
King: I solemnly promise so to do.	*King:* I solemnly promise so to do.
Archbishop: Will you to your power cause Law and Justice, in Mercy, to be executed in all your judgements?	*Archbishop:* Will you to your power cause Law and Justice, in Mercy, to be executed in all your judgements?
King: I will.	*King:* I will.
Archbishop: Will you to the utmost of your power maintain the Laws of God, the true profession of the Gospel, and the Protestant Reformed Religion established	*Archbishop:* Will you to the utmost of your power maintain the Laws of God and the true profession of the Gospel? *Will you to the utmost of your power maintain in*

75

by law ? And will you maintain and preserve inviolably the settlement of the Church of England, and the doctrine, worship, discipline, and government thereof, as by law established in England ? And will you preserve unto the Bishops and Clergy of England, and to the Churches there committed to their charge, all such rights and privileges, as by law do or shall appertain to them, or any of them ?

the United Kingdom[1] *the Protestant Reformed Religion established by law ?* And will you maintain and preserve inviolably the settlement of the Church of England, and the doctrine, worship, discipline, and government thereof, as by law established in England ? And will you preserve unto the Bishops and Clergy of England, and to the Churches there committed to their charge, all such rights and privileges, as by law do or shall appertain to them, or any of them ?

King: All this I promise to do.

(The Bible to be brought)

The things which I have here before promised, I will perform, and keep.

So help me God.

King: All this I promise to do.

(The Bible to be brought)

The things which I have here before promised, I will perform and keep.

So help me God.

It will be seen that the changes were at once sensible and save for the omission of the words 'Statutes in Parliament agreed on' of no very great consequence. But it was none the less disreputable of the Baldwin administration to tamper with the Oath merely on their own responsibility. The Cabinet were the last people who should have interfered in this matter. The object our ancestors had in establishing the statutory Oath was to regulate the exercise of the Royal Prerogative, in which matter, under a constitutional monarchy, the Cabinet are both the Crown's advisers and the executants of policy. By arbitrarily altering the terms of the Coronation Oath without any Parliamentary sanction, the 1937 Cabinet presumed to alter, by their own action, the very bedrock of the authority by which they held their offices.

Further changes are needed in the Coronation Oath this year as a result of the recent Conference of Commonwealth Prime Ministers in London, when the terms of the Queen's styles and titles were once more altered. At the Prime Ministers' Conference each member of the Commonwealth agreed to carry the appropriate legislation for altering the styles and titles through their respective Parliaments and a Bill to achieve this purpose will

[1] Scottish opinion was responsible for underlining the fact that the Oath applied to the United Kingdom and not merely to England.

76

Westminster Abbey and St James's from Charing Cross in the year 1660

An Antient View of St. James's, Westminster Abbey, & Hall, &c *from the Village of* Charing, *near* Charing Cross.

1 St James's Palace.
2 A Public House at the Village of Charing.
3 Westminster Abbey.
4 Westminster Hall.
6 Fields near St James's Park.
7 A Conduit supposed standing

shortly be introduced into the British Parliament. The new styles and titles by which the Queen will be known in Britain are as follows:

> Elizabeth the Second, by the Grace of God of the United Kingdom of Great Britain and Northern Ireland and of her other Realms and Territories, Queen, Head of the Commonwealth, Defender of the Faith.

Again, as in 1937, the changes are not of very great substance but it is understood that Her Majesty's Government, as at present advised, do not intend to amend the Coronation Oath Act. Such a neglect would indeed be deplorable and it would be strange if the present Prime Minister, who was a member of Mr Asquith's Cabinet which altered the Coronation Oath Act by due process of law, and who was not a member of Mr Baldwin's Cabinet which preferred to alter the Oath by its own fiat, should follow the latter rather than the former example. In 1937 Archbishop Lang administered an illegal Oath to King George VI at the very moment when he was conjuring the King to respect the laws of the realm. It seems unthinkable that Archbishop Fisher should allow himself to be coerced into a similarly unlawful role at the Coronation of Queen Elizabeth II. There has been much vacillation as to the exact words of the new Oath and, as this book goes to press, no final decision has been taken. Any change, however, will certainly be illegal unless it is incorporated in an Act of Parliament.[1]

---

[1] As this book was going through the press, it was announced that Her Majesty's Government did not propose to introduce legislation to revise the Oath.

King William III and Queen Mary II

CHAPTER 14

THE COMMONWEALTH AND THE CORONATION

Disappointment has been expressed in some quarters that representatives of the Commonwealth nations have not been invited to carry any of the Queen's Regalia at the coronation. A cogent argument for such an innovation was put forward last year by Mr Dermot Morrah in *The Round Table*. However, no Commonwealth Government has supported this suggestion and there are certainly some who would oppose it if it were advanced in official circles. Indeed, though those who have advanced this proposal have as their objective the strengthening of the unity of the Commonwealth, the very opposite would be the likely outcome.

The constitutional evolution of the Commonwealth is today in a critical stage. Napoleon once said that a constitution should be 'brief and obscure'. Any attempt at this stage to define certain matters with undue precision would only create unnecessary difficulties in one or other of the countries of the Commonwealth. In the past the British constitutional doctrine has been that the Crown is one and indivisible and that the Sovereign, by succeeding to the throne of the United Kingdom, automatically becomes the Sovereign of all the Commonwealth nations. In some of the Commonwealth countries, however, there has grown up a doctrine that there are seven crowns and seven kingdoms and that the Queen is Queen of Canada and Queen of Australia, just as much as she is Queen of the United Kingdom.

Some Commonwealth countries, notably South Africa and to a lesser extent Canada, may feel that if they participated in what after all must remain essentially an English ceremony, they would be conceding part of the doctrine which they have been evolving about the monarchy. Moreover, India which is a republic would certainly not agree (quite apart from the differences of religion) for their representatives to play any role in the ritual. It seems plain that a proposal which was intended to unite opinion would in fact only serve to underline and sharpen existing differences which no one has any interest to stress at this time.

Notwithstanding the above, the High Commissioners of the

Commonwealth countries will, with the exception of India, carry the standards of their countries in procession in the Abbey as they did at the coronation of King George VI in 1937. And all the Commonwealth Prime Ministers, including Mr Nehru from India, will drive in the outdoor procession and also process together inside the Abbey.

Though the Commonwealth Governments have not wished to be more personally identified with the service than in previous years, there has been a greater demand than ever from all the Commonwealth countries for seats, both in the Abbey and on the route. Great efforts have been made to meet these demands. By the exclusion of dowager peeresses and minor peers, by imposing on the general body of the peers a ballot (which some of them deem unconstitutional) to reduce their numbers and by halving the attendance of the schoolboys of Westminster, additional space has been made available and the representatives of the Commonwealth in the Abbey will be nearly twice as numerous as last time when more than 1,000 seats will be reserved for them.

Roughly the same has been done with seating accommodation on the route. One third of all the seats in the official stands will be allocated to the Commonwealth High Commissioners and the Colonial Office for distribution among visitors from the Commonwealth and Colonial Empire.

The Governors-General of the Commonwealth countries will not attend the coronation. They remain in their own countries and, as the Queen's representatives, will be responsible for presiding over ceremonies which will be organised in their own capitals to mark coronation day. Thus it will be true to say that the coronation of 1953 will be world-wide. Apart from the numerous and distinguished representatives of the Commonwealth gathered in the Abbey and along the route, millions of others all over the world will have their own celebrations and there will be no moment in the twenty-four hours of the 2nd June when the Queen's coronation in London will be unaccompanied by religious and military ceremonies thousands of miles away which will mark the unwritten and undefined though genuine unity of the many lands and peoples who acknowledge Queen Elizabeth either as their Queen or as Head of the Commonwealth.

CHAPTER 15

SCOTLAND AND THE CORONATION

The coronation service and ceremony are essentially British institutions and on June 2 the Queen will be crowned at Westminster Queen of the United Kingdom. Since the Act of Union in 1707 in the reign of Queen Anne, England and Scotland have been one kingdom. The Queen's sovereignty over her 'other Realms and Territories' does not require further coronation services to make it valid.

No sovereign has been crowned in Scotland since King Charles II was crowned at Scone in 1651 shortly after he had returned from France and just before his defeat at the Battle of Worcester. However, Scotland still cherishes her own Regalia known as the 'Honours of Scotland'. The Honours consist of the crown, the sceptre and the sword of state. The crown is of gold and is set with twenty-two large gems. The sceptre is of silver gilt ornamented with thistles, fleurs-de-lys, dolphins and Apostles and is surmounted with a globe of rock crystal. The sword of state is over five feet long and has gold etchings of St Paul and St Peter on the sword blade.

The Honours of Scotland have a romantic history. At the time of the Act of Union, which expressly provided that they were to remain in Scotland for all time, they disappeared. The Scots, remembering how Edward I had taken away the Stone of Scone, hid them and, after more than a century, no one knew what had become of them. Then in the early part of the nineteenth century Sir Walter Scott got on the track of them. He deduced that they were locked up in an old chest in the Crown Room in Edinburgh Castle. He obtained a Royal Warrant authorising the opening of the chest. This was done before a distinguished company. 'The chest', wrote Sir Walter, 'seemed to return a hollow and empty sound to the strokes of the hammer. The joy was therefore extreme . . . when the Regalia were discovered lying at the bottom covered with linen cloths, exactly as they had been left in the year 1707.'

Since then the Honours of Scotland have been carefully looked after in Edinburgh Castle where they are on display in a glass case.

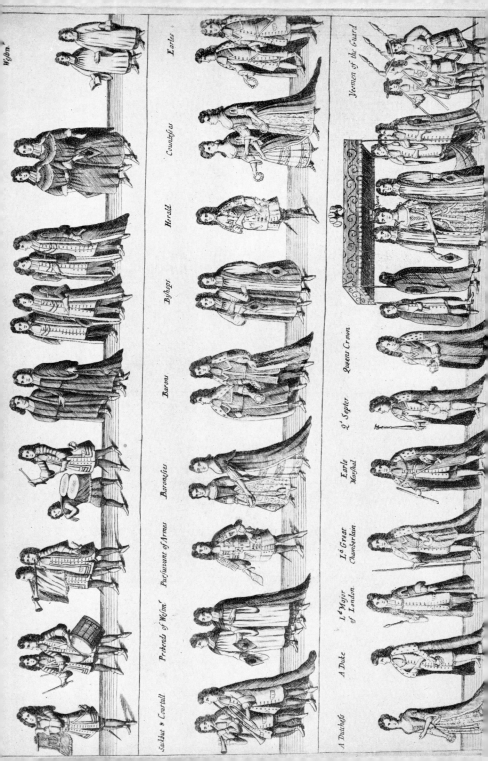

During the last war the Honours of Scotland were once more buried. Only three men, one of whom was Mr P. J. Rose, the King's Remembrancer, knew the spot in Edinburgh Castle where they were walled up to preserve them from damage in air raids. When the Queen visits Scotland she is to attend a National Service on June 24 in St Giles Cathedral where four hundred years ago John Knox vituperated against Mary Queen of Scots. The Honours of Scotland will be carried from the Castle to Holyroodhouse, and thence, in accordance with the old Scottish ceremonial, borne in state before the Queen in a progress from Holyroodhouse to St Giles Cathedral and in solemn procession will be borne before the Queen in the Cathedral.

At the coronation itself, a number of distinguished Scots will take part in the Abbey Procession. Thus Lord Dudhope the hereditary standard bearer, will carry the Scottish standard; the Duke of Buccleuch and the Earl of Home will carry two of the Swords; the Earl of Crawford and Balcarres will act as deputy to the Duke of Rothesay as Great Steward of Scotland; the Duke of Richmond and Gordon will carry the Rod with the Dove; and the Lord High Steward, who will carry St Edward's Crown, will be Viscount Cunningham of Hyndhope.

In addition to Lord Dudhope as hereditary standard bearer, another Scottish family will be represented in the coronation procession by hereditary right. The Lord High Constable of Scotland has, ever since the Act of Union, walked in a prominent position in the Abbey procession. The Countess of Erroll is the 23rd holder of the title which dates back to 1452. She is also 27th Lord High Constable of Scotland an office held in her family since 1314 and is the 32nd Chief of the Hays who trace the chieftainship of the Clan back to 1171. Women, except for Queens, have never taken any leading part in coronations; so this year Lady Erroll applied to the Court of Claims to attend 'by Sufficient Deputy to be approved of by Her Majesty'. The claim was accepted and she will be represented by her uncle Lord Kilmarnock who will carry a Silver Baton tipped with gold with the Royal Arms engraved upon it.

Apart from Scots who take part in the actual coronation procession, Scotland will be represented by the Scottish Members of both Houses of Parliament and by representatives of the judiciary, the Church of Scotland, local authorities and many other bodies. Also representing Scotland at the coronation will be Lord Lyon

Queen Anne's Procession

King of Arms, Sir Thomas Innes of Learney. The Scottish Heralds, Albany, Marchmont and Rothesay, and Dingwall, Unicorn and Carrick Pursuivants, and Falkland Pursuivant-Extraordinary will also take part in the procession. North of the Tweed Lord Lyon is the opposite number of Garter King of Arms, but by reason of his office incorporating that of High Sennachie of the Celtic Kings, which includes a number of the ceremonial functions that in England devolve on the Earl Marshal, he also fulfills most of the ceremonial functions which the Duke of Norfolk as Earl Marshal discharges in England. Unlike Garter, Lord Lyon is a salaried servant of the Queen and he is appointed by the Queen on the advice of the Secretary of State for Scotland. However, with typical Scottish economy, so far from being a dead weight on the taxpayer, he manages to run his ancient Court of Lord Lyon with little cost to the Treasury of the United Kingdom.

The Scots are a far-flung people. Most of the revenue earned by Lord Lyon and his assistants comes from the numerous members of the Scottish clans, who are scattered all over the world, but who write to Lord Lyon in increasing numbers demanding that their pedigrees shall be traced. The Lord Lyon has hitherto walked in the Queen Consort's procession and not with the other Kings of Arms, Garter, Clarenceux, Norroy and Ulster. The uniform of Lord Lyon differs from that of Garter principally in that on Lyon's tabard the Royal Arms appear in their Scottish quartering – with the Scottish lion in the first and fourth quarters, and the English leopard in the second.

There is a small but vocal section of Scottish Nationalists and Scottish Republicans who are now advancing the view that though the Queen is now by inheritance Queen of the United Kingdom at and after the coronation on June 2 she will by being crowned in England with purely English rites and with the English crown, automatically cease to be Queen of the United Kingdom and that Scotland will thereby automatically become an independent Republic. This view finds little support and is strongly opposed by the majority of Scots who, though they have much sympathy with some aspects of Scottish Nationalism, are firmly attached to the Union. They maintain that the Queen succeeded to the throne and will be crowned as Queen of Great Britain. She will moreover be crowned while seated on the Stone of Scone, the ancient coronation seat of all the Kings of Scotland.

The viewpoint of Scottish Unionists may perhaps be summarised as follows: – the Queen will be crowned in that part of Great Britain called England and with that part of the Sovereign's Regalia which is kept and is most conveniently available for a British coronation which takes place in that part of the Kingdom. The Queen could be legally crowned Queen of Great Britain with any part of the Regalia which apertains to any part of the Kingdom. Such a coronation would be an investiture covering all her other realms. Although comprising England and Scotland the United Kingdom is from its very name, one realm and for that reason any of the United Kingdom's symbols of investiture are sufficient. The ceremony at Westminster will take place under the control of the Earl Marshal who is the proper person to control the ceremonies, as the Archbishop of Canterbury is the proper ecclesiastical personage to perform the ecclesiastical parts of a ceremony taking place in the southern portion of the Kingdom.

Some Scots maintain that if it should be the Sovereign's pleasure, or in any way more convenient, perhaps in time of war, for a coronation to be held in some remoter part of the Kingdom, then that ceremony might well be held in Scotland. In such a case Scotsmen would hold that the coronation should take place according to the rites of the Church of Scotland and that the Scottish instead of the English Regalia should be used. The Moderator of the Church of Scotland would preside over the ecclesiastical rites in place of the Archbishop of Canterbury and the rest of the proceedings would be managed by the Lord Lyon and not by the Earl Marshal. A constitutional theory which might well find wide acceptance on both sides of the Tweed is that the coronation might occur in either Scotland or England with the Regalia and ceremonial appropriate to either part of the Kingdom, but that in practice it has been found more generally convenient for the ceremony to take place in England.

CHAPTER 16

THE PLANNING OF THE CORONATION

Coronations are in the nature of things extremely hard to organise. They occur at distant and irregular intervals and each time a machine must be improvised to handle the thousand and one complex problems which arise. There were only three coronations in the nineteenth century, those of George IV, William IV and Victoria. The coronation of Queen Elizabeth II is the fourth of the twentieth century and that of George VI was only sixteen years ago; thus many who played a part in the organisation last time are available with their experience today. On the other hand, the increasing complexity of the modern world brings new problems to each coronation, the greatest single innovation this time being television.

Another difficulty is that a coronation raises everyone's enthusiasm and interest in such things to a very high degree; but after the day itself, there is an inevitable reaction. Therefore, instead of having a series of meetings and conferences after it is over to see in what way it could be amended to the best advantage, or otherwise improved, for 'next time', the inclination is to forget all about it and do no more than offer congratulations all round on its success.

Moreover, with a newly crowned sovereign on the throne, it would be somewhat unseemly to plan for his or her demise, especially as the sovereign would presumably have to be consulted. It is in a way rather like a war. Directly it is over the only thought (especially of those who have been in the thick of it) is to get demobilised and go home as quickly as possible.

In the past, coronations were organised by a Coronation Commission of the Privy Council which delegated most of its powers to a Coronation Executive Committee. For the 1937 coronation, however, a parallel structure was set up so that the Commonwealth could play its full part in the organisation. Thus there came into being the Coronation Commission which this year is presided over by the Duke of Edinburgh. Under the Coronation Commission is the Coronation Joint Committee. The Duke of Norfolk is the

Chairman of both the Coronation Joint Committee and the Coronation Executive Committee.

The Coronation Commission has 39 members, the Coronation Committee of the Privy Council 41 members, the Coronation Joint Committee 34 members and the Coronation Executive Committee 28 members. This massive framework would scarcely be able to function were it not for the fact that most of those who do the real spadework sit on more than one of the Committees. Co-ordination is largely achieved through the fact that Sir Robert Knox, a senior Treasury official, is the secretary of both Commissions and both Committees, a quadruple role which he discharged in 1937. At the last coronation the greater part of the work was done by the Coronation Executive Committee. This year the Commonwealth has shown an increasing desire to share in the planning; the main work has, therefore, been done by the Coronation Joint Committee. This Committee is made up as follows:

Duke of Norfolk .. Earl Marshal

The Archbishop of Canterbury

Sir Alan Lascelles	Private Secretary to the Queen
Lord Tryon	Keeper of the Privy Purse
Hon. Sir Piers Legh ..	Master of the Household
Hon. Sir Albert Napier ..	Permanent Secretary, Lord Chancellor's Department
Hon. Sir George Bellew ..	Garter King of Arms
Sir Percivale Liesching	Permanent Under-Secretary of State, Commonwealth Relations Office
Sir Thomas Lloyd	Permanent Under-Secretary of State, Colonial Office
Sir Terence Nugent ..	Comptroller, Lord Chamberlain's Office
Sir Harold Scott	Commissioner of Metropolitan Police
Sir Harold Emmerson	Permanent Secretary, Ministry of Works
Sir David Milne	Permanent Under-Secretary of State, Scottish Office
Sir John Lang	Permanent Secretary, Admiralty
Sir James Barnes	Permanent Under-Secretary of State, Air Ministry

Sir Frank Newsam	Permanent Under-Secretary of State, Home Office
Sir George Turner	Permanent Under-Secretary of State, War Office
Sir Dermot Kavanagh ..	Crown Equerry
Very Rev. A. C. Don ..	Dean of Westminster
Sir James Crombie	Third Secretary, H.M. Treasury
Air Vice-Marshal N. S. Allinson	Director-General of Personnel, Air Ministry
Mr H. A. Strutt	Assistant Under-Secretary of State, Home Office
Major-General M. B. Dowse	Director of Personal Services, War Office
Mr R. E. Barclay	Assistant Under-Secretary of State, Foreign Office
Mr J. R. Colville	Private Secretary to the Prime Minister
Lieut.-Colonel J. M. Hugo ..	Ceremonial and Reception Secretary, Commonwealth Relations Office
Mr F. J. Fernau	Clerk of the Privy Council
Dr A. L. Geyer	High Commissioner for the Union of South Africa
Mr E. A. P. Wijeyeratne ..	High Commissioner for Ceylon
Hon. Sir Thomas White ..	High Commissioner for the Commonwealth of Australia
Mr F. W. Doidge	High Commissioner for New Zealand
Mr M. A. H. Ispahani ..	High Commissioner for Pakistan
Mr N. A. Robertson ..	High Commissioner for Canada
Sir Robert Knox	H.M. Treasury (Secretary to the Committee)

The number of departments and governments represented above gives some idea of the variety of topics and problems which have to be disposed of. Questions both great and small arise in hordes. Often those which seem the least important prove the most troublesome. How many extra seats should be provided for the Commonwealth? Which categories of persons who have a traditional right to be there shall be eliminated or reduced in numbers to make room for others? Peers? Peeresses? Dowagers? Eldest sons of peers? Peers who are under age? Baronets? If peers cannot be lured outside the Abbey by the promises of free seats in Parliament Square, shall their numbers be reduced by a ballot? If so, ought members of the House of Commons to be reduced in the same proportion? Perhaps they will say that the electorate have already balloted for them and that in this modern age they have more right to be present than the peers. Shall Lord Mayors be allowed to bring their wives? Would it be better to have a few Mayors with their wives, or twice as many Mayors without?

Meanwhile the Archbishop of Canterbury has been wrestling with another set of problems. Shall the coronation ceremony stick to the traditional ritual or should the Moderator of the Church of Scotland be allowed to offer a prayer or preach a sermon? And if so, how about the Free Churches, and the Moslems and Hindus, who are part of the Commonwealth? Shall part of their liturgy be grafted on to the existing ritual?

Are there to be changes in the coronation oath? If so will they require legislation? How much of the ceremony shall be televised? What happens if it rains? Suppose a member of the royal family should die a week before the coronation? Should and could the ceremony be postponed?

How many police will be needed? How many troops are available for lining the route? Can sailors take their place if disturbances abroad make it impossible to bring home troops earmarked for a particular role? These questions have only to be posed for anyone to see the impossibility of answering them to the satisfaction of all. And with so large a committee it is certain that there will always be several points of view. Moreover all the main recommendations of the Joint Committee go to the Cabinets of all the Commonwealth countries for their opinion before they go up to the Coronation Commission, where they receive a further scrutiny.

Only the good sense of all concerned has made it possible to take the requisite decisions in sufficient time. Fortunately the cumberous nature of the organisation was appreciated in advance and preparations for the coronation began in April last year, within a few weeks of the Queen's accession. It is unlikely that the best decision has been taken in every case, but no one can suggest that every idea and point of view has not received fair consideration or that any likely source of muddle or mismanagement has been overlooked.

One of the questions to which the two Committees and the two Commissions have given virtually no attention, is that of expense. However, the Chancellor, Mr Butler, and his vigilant Treasury officials are keeping a close eye on this. It is a fact that up to the end of January no money had so far been voted by Parliament and no reliable estimate of the total cost was available. With the exception of that of William IV every coronation for the last 130 years has been more expensive than the one before. Here is a comparison:

King George IV	..	£243,000
King William IV	..	£ 43,000
Queen Victoria	..	£ 70,000
King Edward VII	..	£125,000
King George V	..	£185,000
King George VI	..	£400,000
Queen Elizabeth II	..	£1,000,000 (at least)

These figures do not tell a story of mounting extravagance, but of the world's entry into the age of inflation. Today the £ barely buys what 2s did in the reign of William IV.

The key figure in the whole planning of the coronation has been the Duke of Norfolk. Neither at school nor when he first joined The Blues was he thought to show signs of much ability, but when in 1937 at the age of twenty-nine it fell to him, as hereditary Earl Marshal, to organise the coronation of King George VI, he soon showed he had gifts of judgment and decision of a very high order. The experience and self-confidence he acquired at the last coronation have served him well in planning this one. Several members of the Coronation Joint Committee have spoken of his outstanding ability as a chairman of a committee. One civil servant whose lot it has been to serve in his time on scores of different committees told the author that without exception the Duke of Norfolk was the best chairman of a committee under whom he had ever sat.

Not the least of the Duke of Norfolk's assets is his imperturbability in the face of ignorant and malicious criticism. The Beaverbrook Press, in the course of its campaign to sabotage the coronation, has sought to represent him as 'on the run' or 'in a dither'. That is certainly not the impression he has made on those who have worked with him in organising the coronation, or even on the General Manager of one of the 'Express' newspapers who was foolish enough to accost him at a large private gathering and retired badly worsted from the encounter.

CHAPTER 17

THE COLLEGE OF ARMS

The main staff on whom the Earl Marshal depends in organising the coronation are the officers of the College of Arms. This is a chartered corporation consisting of the Officers of Arms. They were first incorporated by Richard III in 1484. Their charter, however, soon became inoperative and it was not until 1555 that Queen Mary I granted a new charter which is still in force and made over to them Derby House which is still the site of the College. But heralds and heraldry have a far more ancient history than the College. They are first heard of about the year 1170 and their functions then were to proclaim the names of the champions in the mediaeval tournaments. Mr Anthony Wagner, Richmond Herald, in his book 'Heraldry in England' says

> To cry a knight's name they must first know it. When his helm was closed they could only do so by his arms, and so must be learned in coat armour. Their duties at tournaments grew to keeping scores and interpreting rules and, as tournaments grew more ceremonious, to marshalling both this and other chivalric pageantry. They became a sort of professors of chivalry. From crying jousts they rose to carrying defiance and messages in war with the sacrosanct status of ambassadors.

In early days not only kings but great nobles had their own heralds and pursuivants, who were a lower rank of herald. The Earl of Northumberland's pursuivant derived his name from his master's motto Esperance, while the Duke of Gloucester's pursuivant was named Blanch Sanglier from his master's badge, the white boar. Heraldry, which today is largely a romantic or antiquarian pursuit, was originally of great functional importance. Sir Gerald Wollaston, Ulster and Norroy King of Arms, in a paper which he read to the Society of Arts some years ago, when he was Garter King of Arms, said:

> The object of Heraldry is primarily to distinguish a person by means of symbols clearly recognisable. In its origin it fulfilled this function both in war and peace. In the military system founded by William the Conqueror, and continued throughout the Middle Ages, based on feudal tenure, the tenants-in-chief were bound to attend the sovereign in his wars and to bring with them men-at-arms who were likewise bound to them by sub-infeudation. . . . It was therefore essential that every leader should be clearly recognisable by his retainers. As steel

armour developed, enclosing not only the body but even the face of the knight, some outward symbol of his identity became indispensable. It was also necessary that this should be easily distinguished at a distance. Hence arose the necessity for the heraldic rule that colour must not be placed on colour, nor metal on metal.

It is widely thought that the College of Arms has the right to grant and control arms. This in fact is not so. The right is part of the Royal Prerogative and is delegated by the Sovereign to the Kings of Arms individually according to their respective jurisdictions. And the Kings of Arms as individuals, no less than the College of Arms as an institution, operate under the supervising control of the Earl Marshal, the Duke of Norfolk.

There were originally three Kings of Arms, Norroy north of the Trent, Clarenceux south of the Trent and March in the west country. March disappeared in the fifteenth century and his province was divided between the other two.

In 1417, two years after the Battle of Agincourt, Henry V created the new office of Garter King of Arms. The new appointment had a double significance. Garter was to be the King of Arms of the Order of the Garter and also the Principal King of Arms in England with authority over the provincial Kings. Unfortunately the division of power between Garter and the other Kings of Arms was so ill-defined that in the next three hundred years wordy warfare raged between these competing authorities.

Today the public functions of the College of Arms are restricted to little more than coronations, State openings of Parliament, Royal proclamations of peace, and accessions of Sovereigns, services of the Order of the Garter and the introduction of new peers into the House of Lords. But their principal activity and the source of most of their livelihood is the tracing and verification of pedigrees and coats of arms.

In the last five centuries the College of Arms has recorded or granted arms for about thirty thousand families or persons all of whose male descendants are entitled to a claim to bear such arms. The College of Arms and its members receive no emoluments from public funds; they earn a modest living by charging fees to people who write in from all over the world requiring information about their arms or ancestry.

The earliest seal showing an heraldic shield dates back to 1136. But in an ancient chronicle it is recorded that when Henry I knighted his son-in-law Geoffrey Plantagenet, Count of Anjou in

1127 on the occasion of his marriage, he hung about his neck a shield embellished with golden lions. And there is happily visual confirmation of this. The Count of Anjou, from whom were descended the Plantagenet Kings of England, died in 1151 and was buried in Le Mans Cathedral. In the museum at Le Mans there is preserved a contemporary portrait of him in enamel. This was formerly fixed to his tomb and depicts him holding a shield charged with several rampant golden lions.

The present site of the College (Old Derby House, a former residence of the Earls of Derby, which formerly stood upon it) is in Queen Victoria Street. Old Derby House was burnt down in the Great Fire of 1666, but the Heralds' records were saved and, until the rebuilding was complete, were kept in the Palace of Westminster.

The Chapter of the College of Arms appointed one of its members, Francis Sandford, Rouge Dragon, who was a surveyor and who had been appointed by the King immediately after the Fire, jointly with Wenceslaus Holler, to survey the City as it then stood, to make a 'modell', or plan, of the new College, and to supervise the builder, Morris Emmot, and the work generally. By 1670 Sandford had prepared the 'modell' and Emmot had made a ground 'plott' and the rebuilding began.

In 1672 the Court Room was built. Here as elsewhere in the rebuilding of London, finance was a great difficulty. Fees to the value of upwards of £500 were allocated towards the cost of building, but this was insufficient. Accordingly a Commission was sought from the King, and in 1672 granted, to empower the College to collect subscriptions from the Nobility and Gentry, and in gratitude for such as became benefactors, the College was to register in vellum books their Arms and pedigrees. Two such *Benefactors Books* were completed. One represents donations of £509 5s 6d and the other of £206 6s 8d.

The same year work was begun on the west side, and in 1674 the Library was finished and the books and Records moved to it from Westminster; but in 1677 the building was at a standstill for want of funds. The completion was made possible only by the generosity of the Kings of Arms, Sir William Dugdale, Garter, and Sir Henry St George, Clarenceux. Dugdale built the north-west corner at his own expense, and St George contributed £530 in addition.

In 1683 the north and west sides were complete, comprising

about 40 rooms besides the Porter's Lodge. In 1687 the greater part of the east and south sides being still unbuilt, a sixty-one year building lease for their completion (of a design answerable to the west side) was granted to one Beacham, a stone cutter. The three houses built by Beacham came back into the Heralds' hands in 1748 and continued to be let out on successive short leases until 1866 when the curtailment of the south side of the College, through the construction of Queen Victoria Street, made it necessary to incorporate what remained of them into the College building. The present Record Room was built in 1842 and 1843 as a fireproof repository for the Records, the architect being Robert Abraham.

The Court Room is known as the Earl Marshal's Court having been formerly used for Sittings of the Court of Chivalry. The Royal Arms over the carved throne show that the work was completed about 1707. The fine carving in the Public Office (formerly the Library) is the work of William Emmot, brother of Morris Emmot the builder. Detailed accounts of the seventeenth-century rebuilding are preserved.

CHAPTER 18

THE OUTDOOR PROCESSION

The route of the Queen's procession from Buckingham Palace to the Abbey via the Mall, Trafalgar Square, Northumberland Avenue, Victoria Embankment and Parliament Square is one mile and three-quarters long. The great State Coach, which weighs 4 tons, might get out of control if the horses were allowed to trot; so the procession will move at a walking pace of $3\frac{1}{5}$ miles an hour. At this rate the procession to the Abbey will take just over half an hour.

The return route after the ceremony is a far more prolonged undertaking, the distance to be traversed being 5 miles 250 yards, and will take little short of two hours. The Queen will drive down Whitehall to Trafalgar Square, then via Cockspur Street, Pall Mall, St James's Street and Piccadilly to Hyde Park Corner. From there her procession will go by the East Carriage Drive parallel with Park Lane, turn right at Marble Arch, down Oxford Street and Regent Street to Piccadilly Circus. From there she will drive down the Haymarket, Cockspur Street and Trafalgar Square, pass once more under Admiralty Arch and so home to Buckingham Palace down the Mall.

Something like 20,000 sailors, soldiers and airmen will line the route and an equal number of Police will be on duty. The Metropolitan Police are seriously under strength and 5,000 Police from the provinces will be drafted in to provide the necessary force. With so much of the Army overseas and with a longer route then ever, the Navy and the Air Force will be drawn on more than at previous coronations and for the first time the stratagem of a 'stage navy' will be introduced in order to eke out the slender force. The sailors and cadets who line the Victoria Embankment during the outward procession will, during the Abbey ceremony, march through New Scotland Yard and take up new positions in Whitehall for the return journey.

The stands which are being erected by the Ministry of Works along the route will provide seating accommodation for 135,000 people. It is probable that a similar number of people will be able to get a first-class view from buildings along the route. The Government departments in Whitehall, the shipping offices in Cockspur Street, the clubs in Pall Mall, St James's Street and Piccadilly, the great hotels in Park Lane and the department stores in Oxford Street and Regent Street provide from their windows and roofs magnificent vantage points. The Police estimate that 435,000 people will be able to stand with comfort and safety on the pavements. Thus the total number of people who can see the procession directly with their own eyes will be in the neighbourhood of 700,000. Twenty or thirty times that number will probably be gathered around the nation's two million television sets.

One of the incalculable factors about the coronation is what effect television will have upon the crowds in the street. Scotland Yard take the view that the biggest London crowds are drawn by funerals; second in drawing power are Royal weddings with coronations a close third. The crowds in the streets for the funeral of the late King were much smaller than was expected, but it is hard to tell whether the principal factor was the disagreeable weather or the drawing power of television. It may well be found that this year television will steal the crowds. Many people may prefer to see both the Abbey ceremony and the outdoor procession in the comfort of their homes rather than to see only the outdoor procession from the pavement. On the other hand, there are always those who like the excitement of being part of a crowd.

Before the Queen's procession sets out from Buckingham Palace at 10.26, there will be a number of other processions to occupy the attention of the crowds. First there will be long fleets of motor-cars carrying official guests and members of the Diplomatic Corps. Then will come the procession of Native Rulers followed by that of the Commonwealth Prime Ministers. The Prime Ministers and their wives will ride in nine two-horse Clarences. Each Prime Minister except Mr Nehru will have a mounted escort and, in the case of the British Prime Minister, Mr Churchill, who will be dressed in his resplendent and unique uniform as Lord Warden of the Cinque Ports, the escort will be found by the 4th Hussars in which regiment he served in his youth and of which he is now Colonel-in-Chief. The 4th Hussars have been given special permission to wear their full dress uniform.

Next will come a procession of three State Carriages with members of the Royal Family. The Duchesses of Kent and Gloucester will probably drive together. Then will come the procession of Queen Elizabeth the Queen Mother which will consist of two State Carriages with a Captain's Escort of Household Cavalry carrying her Standard. In the first carriage will be the Queen Mother and Princess Margaret while the Queen Mother's suite will ride in the second.

The Queen's procession will consist of three two-horse State carriages containing her suite and the great State Coach drawn by eight Greys. Ahead of her will ride the Field Marshals, members of the War Office Staff, the Air Council, the Army Council and the Board of Admiralty. Immediately around the Coach will ride the Master of the Horse, the Duke of Beaufort, the Lord High Steward of England, Admiral of the Fleet Viscount Cunningham of Hyndhope and the Lord High Constable of England, Field Marshal Viscount Alanbrooke. The Duke of Edinburgh will ride in the State Coach, sitting on the Queen's left.

Immediately behind the coach will come the Queen's Standard escorted by the Duke of Gloucester and Earl Mountbatten. Included in the Queen's procession will be an escort of officers from Commonwealth and Colonial contingents, the Queen's Bodyguard of the Yeoman of the Guard, the Queen's Bargemaster and twelve Watermen and the massed bands of the Household Cavalry. Her escort will consist of a Sovereign's Escort of the Household Cavalry riding in four divisions.

The whole of the route will be decorated with flags, pennants, canopies and flowers and these decorations will find their counterpart in every city, borough and village in the land. The Royal Borough of Kensington are taking special pains with their decorations. At Palace Gate they intend to erect a mediaeval canopy which will serve as a triumphal arch at the boundary of the borough with the coronation city of Westminster. Decorated with crowns and heraldic symbols in the borough's colours of red and green, it will rise 30 feet above the roadway and should be one of the most impressive sights in London in coronation year.

Those who are not able to see the Queen on coronation day, will have many other opportunities of doing so, as for the two months of June and July the Queen and the Duke of Edinburgh will have an almost daily round of public engagements. A full list of these functions is set out in Appendix D.

CHAPTER 19

H.R.H. THE DUKE OF EDINBURGH

The role of a man who marries a queen cannot be an easy one. A woman who marries a man of more exalted status automatically acquires his rank; while if his status is lower than hers she retains her own. Under English custom, however, a man's status is unaffected by his marriage. Thus any preferment which is given to the husband of a queen can only be the result of the sovereign's wish or the action of Parliament.

The Duke of Edinburgh was born Prince Philip of Schleswig-Holstein-Sonderburg, the branch of the Danish royal family which has sat on the throne of Greece since 1863. Prince Philip was the only son of Prince Andrew, the fourth son of George I of Greece. Nine months before his marriage to Princess Elizabeth, as the Queen then was, he became a naturalised British subject, renounced his Greek royal title and changed his name to Mountbatten, the maiden name of his mother, formerly Princess Alice, the elder daughter of the first Marquess of Milford Haven.

From the moment of his British naturalisation it became incorrect to speak of him as Prince Philip; and it still is. For a short period he was Lieut. Philip Mountbatten, R.N. The day before his marriage to Princess Elizabeth, on 20 November 1947, the late King created him His Royal Highness the Duke of Edinburgh and he thus became a peer of the realm. He did not become, and is not now, a royal Duke. This phrase is a colloquialism used to denote princes of the blood royal, which means the blood royal of England. In the case of a man, birth and birth alone can confer this appellation.

It is everyone's desire that the Queen's husband shall be treated with every proper mark of respect and there was very general satisfaction and approval when on September 30 the Queen removed many grounds for doubt as to the Duke's position and precedence by causing Garter King of Arms to publish the following announcement in the London Gazette:

> The Queen has been graciously pleased by Warrant bearing date the 18th instant to declare and ordain that His Royal Highness Philip, Duke

Sir Henry Dymoke, Champion to King George IV

of Edinburgh, Knight of the Most Noble Order of the Garter, Knight of the Most Ancient and Most Noble Order of the Thistle, Commander in the Royal Navy, shall henceforth upon all occasions and in all Meetings except where otherwise provided by Act of Parliament have, hold and enjoy Place, Pre-eminence and Precedence next to Her Majesty.

This action was very timely because the Queen was due on November 4 to open Parliament in state and it was most desirable that the Duke's position should be clear beyond a doubt. A few days after her accession the Queen made it known to the Royal household that for household purposes the Duke was to rank immediately after herself. In matters of precedence inside the household the Queen acts through and upon the advice of the Lord Chamberlain. All matters of precedence outside the household are regulated by the Earl Marshal on the advice of Garter King of Arms, but there is one proviso to this; and it is to be noted that the announcement in the London Gazette included the words 'except where otherwise provided by Act of Parliament'.

Her Majesty's legal advisers were obviously wise to enter this caveat. It is however to be regretted that having done so they appear to have neglected to consider whether there was in fact any Act of Parliament which did 'otherwise provide'. If they had, they would surely not have advised the Queen to command the Duke of Edinburgh to sit where he did at the State opening of Parliament, for it is clear beyond all question of doubt, that those who caused him to sit in a chair on the left of the Queen transgressed an Act of Parliament, violated the Standing Orders of the House of Lords and flew in the face of the Queen's own Royal Warrant of September 30.

Let it at once be plain that no kind of fault attaches to the Duke of Edinburgh. Ever since his marriage he has shown a most becoming modesty and has exerted himself to ensure that no action of his could even by implication be thought presumptuous. In such matters, he can only act upon the Queen's commands and Her Majesty can only act upon advice. If the advice is faulty it is the advisers who are to blame. There is therefore no reason why this intricate and delicate matter should not be ventilated; and many reasons why it should.

An Act of King Henry VIII entitled 'An Acte for the placing of the Lordes in the Parliamt' which was placed on the Statute book in 1539 is the one which the Queen's legal advisers should have had in their minds. This Act not only has the authority of

Queen Victoria in her Coronation Robes

antiquity, but it was revised as recently as 1948. The deadwood was then cut out thus giving renewed vitality to those sections which still survived the cold scrutiny of the committee charged with statute law revision.

At the outset of the Act it is laid down that 'onlie the Kinges children' shall sit on 'any side of the clothe of estate'. Until recently most of the officials in the House of Lords thought that the Cloth of Estate was the carpet that covers the platform on which the throne is placed. A technical case could be made that the Duke of Edinburgh by sitting on the Cloth of Estate instead of 'at any side' had not transgressed the law. However, the officials of the House of Lords have now abandoned the carpet theory. Recent research has shown conclusively that the Cloth of Estate was a canopy.[1] When the House of Lords was rebuilt after the fire of 1834, the cloth canopy was not replaced. Peers who on entering the chamber habitually bow to the Cloth of Estate have, in effect, been bowing to something which either no longer exists or which they perhaps hold to be represented by the carved wooden panelling behind and over the throne.

In either case, the position of the Duke of Edinburgh is equivocal: so too is that of eldest sons of peers and Members of Parliament who are Privy Councillors who for many years have habitually sat on the steps of the throne during debates in the House of Lords. The fact that the sovereign is not present on these occasions makes no difference, since the Act says 'whether the Kinges Majestie be there psonallie psent or absent'.

Whatever view may be taken about the Cloth of Estate, and it is a lush field for discussion, there can be no doubt that the Queen's legal advisers have allowed the Duke of Edinburgh to transgress another clause of the same Act. For the Act, after seating the Archbishops, Bishops and Great Officers of the Realm in their appropriate places, goes on to say that everyone else 'shall sytt and be placed after their auncientes as it hathe ben accustomed'. Now the Duke of Edinburgh, not being a Prince of the blood royal, is the junior Duke and ranks immediately after the Duke of Argyll. The Roll of the Lords Temporal and Spiritual published on 12 November 1952 shows that his precedence in the House of Lords is 30, which is exactly what it should be according to the Act of 1539.

Moreover, the Standing Orders of the House of Lords baldly

[1] See Appendix A in the author's *They Serve the Queen*.

state in paragraph 3, 'The Lords are to sit in the same order as is prescribed by the Act of Parliament', and all the relevant portions of the Act are printed in an Appendix. The Act was first included in the Appendix in 1825 and it is still there in the latest edition of Standing Orders published in 1936. Officials who have belatedly discovered these facts have sought to console themselves with two arguments. The first is that the Duke of Edinburgh was seated in the same way as the Prince Consort. Against this it must first be mentioned that the two cases are not on all fours.

Unlike the Duke of Edinburgh the Prince Consort was not a peer. This may make the case of the Prince Consort more serious than that of the Duke of Edinburgh, for it could be argued that he had no right in the House of Lords at all. Alternatively, it could be argued that, as the Prince Consort was not a Peer, the Act did not apply to him.   But in any case, the mere fact that the Prince Consort was wrongly advised to break the law is no reason why the Queen's legal advisers one hundred years later should give equally bad advice. Two blacks don't make a white.

The other argument which is of a far more dangerous character and has, it is believed, been abandoned, is that the matter of precedence is entirely within the royal prerogative and that the Queen acting through the Lord Chancellor and the Lord Great Chamberlain can give such instructions as she pleases as to where the peers shall be seated. This argument will not hold water for a minute and the Queen would indeed be ill-served if such advice were seriously proffered. It is true that in the preamble to the 1539 Act King Henry VIII states that all this is in 'his progatyve royall' but it is an axiomatic part of the British constitution that when a part of the royal prerogative has once been surrendered it cannot be recovered except by due legal process which has in fact never been attempted. And this point has already been conceded by the very terms of the Queen's warrant of 30 September where the words were sagaciously inserted 'except where otherwise provided by Act of Parliament'.

It is plain that something must be done to rectify this situation. If Her Majesty were to be advised that the Duke of Edinburgh should sit beside her at the next opening of Parliament, in addition to the breach of Statute Law and Standing Orders, they would be advising her to break her Coronation Oath in which she swears to uphold the laws of the land. As against all this it is very plain that it would be most unsuitable for the Duke of Edinburgh to occupy so lowly a position as the law dictates when the Queen next opens Parliament. But there is a very simple remedy for the tangled situation: namely to amend the 1539 Act with a one-clause Bill which would provide that in the case of a husband of a Queen regnant, he shall out-rank all other peers.

This in fact was done for Prince George of Denmark, husband of Queen Anne, thirteen years before his wife ascended the throne. At the Coronation of William and Mary, he was created Duke of Cumberland with precedence over all other peers. An Act was put on the Statute Book (1 William & Mary, Session 2, c. 8–9). For the avoidance of any future confusion the revision of the 1539 Act might also say that, notwithstanding anything in the Act, the husband of a Queen regnant is to sit beside her at State Openings of Parliament.

It seems important and desirable that a matter like this should be tidied up in Coronation year. Already there has been a muddle about the titles and styles by which the Queen was proclaimed at her accession. These were contrary to those laid down by the Statute of Westminster of 1936. This admittedly was done in a great hurry and a new formula was devised at short notice to satisfy the views of the Commonwealth. However, when the Queen's styles and titles had to be proclaimed ten days later over the late King's tomb in St George's Chapel, Windsor, it was thought more prudent to proclaim her by the styles and titles provided by the existing law.

Following upon the recent conference of Commonwealth Prime Ministers in London legislation will shortly be introduced into all Commonwealth Parliaments giving legal effect to what was then decided. It is much to be desired that this sensible precedent will be followed and that Parliamentary time will be found in the near future for the necessary and simple legislation to regulate in an equally sensible fashion the parliamentary precedence of the 'first gentleman in the land'.

Queen Victoria leaving Buckingham Palace for her Coronation

APPENDIX A

(i)

LITTLE DEVICE FOR THE CORONATION OF KING HENRY VII

The 'Little Device for the Coronation of Henry VII' was almost certainly compiled two years earlier for the coronation of Richard III in 1483. The writer of this document assumed that a queen would be crowned with the King. In fact, Henry VII, who was crowned in 1485, did not marry Elizabeth of York until three months after his coronation and she was not crowned till 1487.

There are four known manuscript copies of the 'Little Device'. Three are in the British Museum and one in the possession of the Duke of Rutland at Belvoir. This text, which is collated from all four, is taken from 'English Coronation Records' edited by Leopold G. Wickham Legg.

Here followeth vnder correction a little devise of the coronacion of the most high and mightie christian Prince Henrie the vijth[1] rightfull and undoubted Heire and king of the crowne of England and of Fraunce w^t their appurtenunces and by the hole assent of all the Lordes both Spirituall and Temporall, and also of all the Commons of this Lande elect, chosen, and required the xxx^{tie} daye of October Anno Domini MCCCCiiij^{xx}v in London to be king of the same. Also of the most noble Princes dame Elizabeth his wief Lawfull Queene of Englande, and fraunce etc. to be solempnized at Westminster.

Fyrst for that there is required manifolde great and humble services to be don as apperteigneth to the kinges most royall person and estate. And the same services belonge to many, divers, and great Lordes, and other nobells of this his Royalme by enheritaunce and custome. Therfore that the king may assuredly be served, and euery Lorde; and noble person of his Royalme maye vse and enioye such as becometh him by right, The kinges Highnes following Justice hath don to be made his open proclamacions, that euery person clayming to do him any maner service vpon the day of his Coronacion shalbe at the White hall in his Pallice of Westminster the xiiij daye of October next comyng, and hath authorised the Erle of Pembroke, the Erle of Oxenforde, the Lorde Standley,

---

[1] The letter j in the numerals which follow represents i; vij is therefore 7.

The Market Place, Wisbech, on the day of the Coronation of Queen Victoria, when 5,000 persons were regaled with Roast Beef, Plum Puddings and Ale

Sr Edwarde Standley, Sr William Husse to heare and determyne euery mans right in that behalf etc.

Also in avauncing the auncyent nobles of Englande, the king hath appoynted a good numbre of noble persons of this his Royalme to take order of knighthoode, and be made knightes of the bathe in the Tower of London the xxvijth daye of October next comyng called the evyn of his Coronacion. And that all maner of thinges that belong to such a triumph may be done honorably and orderly disposed. The kinges highnes hath ordeined the noble Lorde the Erle of Oxenforde, Chamberlayn of Englande. The Lorde Standley to be Constable of Englande, the Erle of Notingham to be Marshall of Englande for that daye. Yet forasmuch as the solempnitie of the Kinges Coronacion and the Queenes is departed in ij dayes observaunce, that is to wytte next the day of coronacion, which is called the evyn or vigile of the Coronacion. Therfore it is to be shewed following the state behaving and demeaning as well of the King, as of the Queene for thes ij dayes. And first of the King.

The Kinges highnes the xxviijth day of October next being in the Tower of London, and honorably accompani(ed) wth his Lordes after the hearing of his divine seruice the Masse ended, shall come into the hall where shalbe a Siege royall prepared as accordeth for his estate. Wherin his grace sitting, or standing shall order knightes of the Bathe after the forme of the auncient custome of King(es) of Englande. And there in the same place standing great Lordes in such estate, as shalbe thought to his highnes for the hono^r and weale of him and his Roialm(e).

The order of creacion of knightes of the Bathe to be vnderstande by the Herauldes and so to be conveyed &c.

That don the king at his pleaso^r may go to dyner, and that it hath ben accustomed such noble persons as are than made Knightes of the Bathe, in order as thei were made knightes to bere the dishes to the Kinges bourde in ordre.

Afterward thei saye all the Lordes Temporall, the Maio^r of London, thaldermen, herauldes of Armes, Sergeauntes of Armes, trumpettes, mynstrells, and all other officers according are to be warnede to geve their attendaunce at the saide Towre of London by on afternone the daye after. And sone thervpon the King at the saide towre arrayed in a doublet of Grene, or white clothe of golde as long gowne of purple veluet furred w^t Ermyns w^t a riche Sarple and gartes to take his horse trapped w^t a riche trapper, w^t seven corsours following him, all trapped in riche and divers trappers and w^t a spare corsour ladde in hande, trapped w^t a trapper of the Kinges Armes and saddeled w^t Crymsen veluet, except the Kinges own saddle wch is couered w^t like clothe of golde to the saddle of estate and seven henchemen clothed in dowbletts of Crymsen Satten, and in gownes of white clothe of golde to follow the King vpon seven corsours barehedded.

In this wise the king shall ride barehedded vnder a Canapie of clothe of golde bawdken[1] w^t foure staves gilte to be borne allwaye by foure noble knightes, thei to be chaunged at divers and many places aswell for that thei king maye be seruid fo many noble persons to their great hono^r as for their ease that beare it, considering the long distaunce from the towre to westminster.

Afore the king directly, his swearde shalbe borne by a Peere of the Roialme on the right hande of the Swearde the Lorde great Chamberlaine of Englande, on the Left hande of the Swearde the Marshall of Englande. Next before them the Maio^r of London bearing a mace in his hande and Garter knight of tharmes on his right hande, and before them ij Squiers for the kinges bodie, bearing in baudrick wise twoo mantells furred w^t Ermyns, wearing twoo hattes of Estate of Crymsen clothe of golde beked on, beks turnyd vpp behinde, and furred also w^t Ermyns in representacion of the kinges twoo duchesses[2] of Gyen and Normandie. Afore them all the herauldes, and Mynstrells. Afore them the newe made knightes of the Bathe, Afore them other noble men, etc.

Thes so orderid, the kinges highnes, attending vpon him on foote three score knightes, A hundreth Esquiers wearing his Liverie, and yomen of the Crowne and of his chamber in a great numbre, shall ride from the saide Towre by the open streetes of London into Chepe, from thence to fleetestreete, and so directly fourth vnto the kinges great hall in his pallaice at Westminster, etc.

Sone after the king is passed out of the Towre, the Queene shall followe vpon quysshins of white damaske clothe of golde barehedded wearing a rownde circle of golde set w^t pearles and pretious stones arayed in a kirtle of white damaske clothe of golde furred w^t Myniuer pur garnisshed w^t Amblettes of golde, Aboue that a Mantell w^t a trayne of the same white damaske clothe of golde, furred w^t Ermyns sitting in a Lytter w^t out any bayles or covering. Aboue her hed couered w^t white damaske of silke garnesshed w^t

---

[1] A rich stuff, originally woven with woof of silk and warp of gold.
[2] Duchies

fringe of Silke and golde w^t Ryband of gold and gilt nayles w^t iiij
pomells chased and gilte lyned in the bottome w^t lynnen clothe.
twoo great Co^{r}sours bearing the saide Lytter vpon two saddles
couered w^t white damaske clothe of golde garnished w^t fring of
white silke and golde Ryband of the same, twoo dorsers of ledder[1]
couered w^t white damaske clothe of golde lyned w^t white damaske
of silke, twoo bridles, two crowpers,[2] two collers, two paytrells,[3]
w^t two trappers and other their apparell in white damaske of silke,
Alwayes iiij noble knightes bearing a Cele[4] of white damaske Lyned
w^t white Tartaryn[5] vpon shaftes burnished w^t siluer, iiij belles of
latyn[6] fastened to them ouer the queene, thei to be chaunged as it
is aboue said of the king. The Lordes Grey and Powes leading the
horse of the Lytter.

There shall followe the Quene v. henchemen, all clothed in
dowblettes of crymsen Satten, and gownes of blewe veluet ryding
in women saddles couered w^t crymsen clothe of golde. next after
them a palfrey w^t a Saddle of estate couered w^t clothe of golde to
be Ledd spare by the yoman of the Queenes horses. After them
three Cheires w^t xij Ladies therin. The first chaire couered w^t
Crymsen clothe of golde, the second w^t veluet crymsen, the thirde
w^t crymsen damaske. After them vij Ladies all clothed in gownes
of blewe veluet purfelled w^t crymsen Satten sitting on vij palfreys
all of oon colo^r w^t saddles couered w^t Crymsen clothe of golde,
horse harnes of the same in maner and demye trappers cutt flame
wise furred w^t Ermyns powdred etc.

Next after the Queene shall ride her Chamberlain. Afore him
two esquiers vsshers of her chambre, either of them bearing in
bawdrick wise a Mantell furred w^t Ermyns and couered w^t Ermyns. And two hattes of estate of crymsen clothe of golde bek on
beke turned vp behinde and furred w^t Ermyns.

Also there shall ride afore the Queene many Lordes of all estates,
knightes, esquiers, and noble men in great numbre. And about her
person on foote many knightes, esquiers, vsshers and yomen of her
chambre.

In this wise the Queene shall ride following the king till thei
bothe come to Westminster hawle, where thei bothe vnder clothes
of estate at the estende of Westminster halle maye be servid of the
voide.[7]

And that don to be brought into the chambre And for the king

---

[1] Leather.   [2] Cruppers.   [3] Breastpiece.   [4] Canopy.   [5] Kind of satin.
[6] Brass alloy (probably gilt).   [7] A form of spiced wine.

shalbe arrayed a bayne, and he therein to be bayned, which don the king and the quene maye take their rest, and so endeth the observaunce of the evyn of the Coronacion etc.

On sondaye the daye of the coronacion xxx daye of October the king arrayed by Sr Giles dawbeney deputie for that daye Chamberlain in forme following First w^t two shirtes on of Lawne, thother of Crymsen Tartayne both Largely opened before, and behinde, and in the shulders. Laced w^t Amblettes of silver and gilt, A great large breche,[1] belte of velvet to gather the same togither. A paire of hosen of Crymsen Sarsenet vampeys[2] and all. A cote of Crymsen Satten largely openid as the shirtes be to the which cote his hosen shalbe Laced w^t ryband of silke A Sircote close furred w^t menyver pur, wherof the collo^r handes, and the Speres shalbe garnished with Ryband of golde. A hoode of estate furred w^t Mynever pur and purfelled w^t Ermyns. A great mantell of Crymsen Satten furred also w^t mynever pur w^t a great Lace of silke, w^t two tassells also in colo^r crymsen, A Little Cappe of estate of Crymsen satten ermyned and garnisshed w^t ryband of golde. And accompanyed w^t his Lordes temporalls in their robes and noble men shall come early. And it is founden by presidents by vj of the clock from his chambre into Westminster hall where he shall sitt vnder clothe of estate in the marble chaire appareilled w^t clothes and quisshons of clothe of golde bawdekyn as it apperteigneth.

The Queene also then immediately arayed in a smock of Raynes,[3] A Sircote royall of crymsen velvet opened before vnder her wast fastened w^t a Lace of the holie vnction lyned the shulders and furred the bodie w^t Mynever pur garnisshed w^t Amblettes of Siluer and gilte. Aboue that a Mantell of crymsen veluet w^t a Trayne furred w^t Ermyns bearing on her bare hedd a riche Circle of golde, her heare faire lying about her shulders following the king and betwixt her and the king only the Lordes of great estate, as Dukes, and Erles w^t her Chamberlain going before her. on the side half her trayne borne by a great Duches, all the Ladies and gentlewomen arayed in robes of Scarlett furred w^t the Queenes Liuerie, She shall followe the king and be set vnder a clothe of estate somwhat lower then the kinges.

And it is to be remembred, that the kinges Benche, and also the places of the Chauncerye must be apparelled vnder foote vpon the rayles, and along vpon the walles w^t redde worsted. And also that the Marshall of Englande be well apparelled and accompanyed

[1] This comma is probably superfluous. [2] Foot-covering. [3] Cloth from Rheims.

wᵗ men having tipped staves to make a Large wey for the kinges and the queenes procession, and for his retourne. And all the Sergeantes of Armes arayed and accompanyed, as it shall please the king to give their continuall attendaunce for the suertie of the kinges person, and of his Lordes.

The King and the Queene thus set in Sieges royall, and the way from thence vnto the Pulpit in Westminster churche arayed vnder foote wᵗ Ray clothe, by the which somtyme was Beauchampe of Bedforde The Cardinallis Archbushopp of Canturburie Tharchbusshop of York wᵗ other Lordes Spirituall, and all pontifically arayed and the Abbot of Westminster wᵗ his Couent[1] in Copes bearing Reliques and other thinges accustomed to be borne in Coronacion that is to saye, A chalice of gold, a Patene of the same, a Sceptre wᵗ the dove, and an other rodde of golde for the queene shall come vnto the king. And the queene so sitting in Westminster hall, and there by thadvice of the Lordes a solempne procession shalbe set furthe, wherin the king then being bare hedded, and having the busshopp of Exceter to susteyne him on his right hande, and the busshopp of Elye on his Left hande, shall go vnder a Cele of clothe of golde bawdekyn wᵗ iiij staves and foure belles of siluer and gilte. The same to be borne by the baronettes of the five portes wheresoeuer the king go save when he is nigh vnto the high aulter, foure of them alwaye at the bearing of euery staffe. Next before the King my Lorde of worcestre Chauncelloʳ of Englande shall beare the Challice of golde and els some busshopp shalbe appoynted in his place, before him the Treasauroʳ of Englande, if he be a busshop, shall beare the Patene And in case if he be no busshop, then the busshop of Chester to be appoincted in his place by the king. Next to them the duke of Bedforde bearing the kinges crown before him the duke of Suffolke bearing the kinges Sceptre on his right hande of the Crowne, before him the Earle of Arundell bearing the rodde of golde yn the Left hande Before him the Erle of Darbye bearing the kinges Swearde in a Scabard before him iiij Earles going togither, that is to saye, the Erle of Shrewsburie bearing a swearde called Curtana naked. The Erle of devonshire on his right hande bearing an other sweard naked, before them the Erle of Essex bearing the kinges Sporres before him and the newe made knightes of the Bathe in a Liuerey.

In this order the king shall go vpon Raye clothe to be Layed by the Awlmoner from his Siege in the hall to the pulpit through his

---

[1] Convent.

pallaice into Westminster church entering at the west dore, where when the king is well entered, he shall somwhat tarye.

And after that the king as in order aboue the Queene susteyned w^t the busshop of Exceter on her right hande and the busshop of Norwich on her Left hande in steede of the busshop of Duresme and Bathe vnder a Cele of Bawdeken w^t foure staues and iiij belles borne by the barons of the v. portes in fourme as aboue in Chapitre of the king. And next before the queene a crowne to be borne by the Erle of Arundell, before it a Sceptre of golde w^t a dove in the topp to be borne by the viscount Lisle. All the Ladies and gentlewomen next after her shall followe the Lordes and other nobles after them shall followe the king. And when she is at the entrance of the west dore of the churche of Westminster there shalbe saied ouer her by the said Cardinall as Archbusshopp this orison. *Omnipotens sempiterne Deus et cetera.*

Which orison ended, the king and the Queen to procede in fourme and order as aboue through the quere to the pulpit, it to be couered w^t red worsted. In the middes wherin must be two sieges royall of clothe of golde and quisshins of the same arayed by the vsshers of the kinges and queenes chambres. And the king and the Queene to be set in them save it is to wit, that the kinges Siege must be made a good deele hyer then the queenes, wch shall be on the Left hande of the kinges and longer than it.

This done the Cardinall as Archbusshop of Canterbury shewing the king to the people at the iiij partes of the said pulpit, shall say on this wise, Sirs here is present Henry rightfull and indoubted enherito^r by the Lawes of god and man to the Crowne and royall dignities of Englande w^t all thinges therevnto annexid and apperteigning elect chosen and required by all three estates of thissame Lande to take vpon him this said crown and royall dignitie. wher-vpon ye shall vnderstande that this daye is fixed and appoiynted by all the Peres of this Lande for the consecracion, Invnction and coronacion of the said most excellent prince Henry. Will ye Syrs at this tyme give your willes and assentes to the same consecracion, Invnction and Coronacion. wherunto the people shall saye w^t a great voice, yea, yea, yea, so be it, King Henry, King Henry, King Henry.

Sone vpon the said Cardinall as Archbusshop of Canturbury being revesshed as apperteigneth for the celebracion of the masse, and also the forsaid busshoppes of Exeter, and of Ely both sides as aboue w^t other busshops and w^t the Abbot of westminster who oweth alwey to be nigh the King for his enformacion in such things as concerne the solemnpnitie of his crowning. The king shalbe brought honorably from his said Siege vnto the high aulter, where the Chauncello^r of Englande shall set downe the Challice, and in Likewise the busshop of Cheste^r the Patene, The queene following the king thither going afore. the Lordes as aboue bearing her Crown Sceptre and Rodde, and the aboue said busshops systeyning her. And for her there shalbe made on the Left side of the high aulter a folding Stoole. She shall sit while the king be required for the keping of the customes and Lawes of Englande. And that done while, *Veni creator Spiritus* et c. ys in singing, and all the while the king is anoynting she shall knele praying for the king and her-self.

At the whiche aulter the king ought to offer a Pall, and a pownde of golde, and xxiiij which shalbe deliuerid vnto him by the Chamberlayn. And furthew^t the pavement afore the high aulter worshipfully arayed w^t Carpettes and Quisshins the king shall there lye downe groveling whiles the said Cardinall as Arch-busshop seith vpon him. *Deus humilium.* Which done the same Cardinall may at his pleasure commaunde some short service to be said during which season the said Cardinall shall sit before the high aulter his back towardes the same as is accustomed and the king shall sit against him face to face in a chaire prepared as to so high estate accordeth.

The busshopp of Lincolne shall make a Sermon and the service being ended the Cardinall shall aske the king vnder this forme w^t an open and distinct voyce *Will ye graunt and keepe to the people of Englande the Lawes and customes to them as olde rightfull and devoute kinges graunted, and the same ratifie, and confirme by yor other And specially lawes and customes and Liberties graunted to the Clergie, and people by your Predecessors, and glorious king Saynct Edwarde ?* The king shall answere, *I graunt and promit.* And when the king before all the people hath promised trewly to graunte and kepe all thes premmisses, then shall the said Cardinall open vnto him the speciall Articles whervnto the king shalbe sworne the same Cardinall saying as followeth. *Ye shall keepe after your strenght and power the church of god to the Clergie. And the people hoole peace and godlie concorde.* The king shall answere *I shall keepe.*

Ye shall make to be done after your strenght and power rightfull Justice in all your domes and judgementes, and discrecion w^t mercie and trowthe. The king shall answer *I shall do.*

108

The Court of the Lord Lyon

The Officers of the College of Arms

Do ye graunte the rightfull Lawes and customes to be holden and promitte yow after your strenght and power such lawes as to the worship of god shalbe chosen by your people by yow to be streghthenid and defended ? The king shall answer, *I graunte and promitte.*

Then followeth the peticion of the busshop to the king, wch by the busshop of Lincoln shalbe openly redd in a good and distinct voice. saying. *Domine Rex, Sir king, We aske of yo^w to be perfectly geven and graunted vnto vs, that ye shall keepe to vs, and eche of vs the Privileges of the Lawe Canone and of holie church and dewe Lawes and rightfulnes, and vs and them defende as a devout and christian king owght to do. And in Likewise to do and graunte throughout all yor Realme to euery busshop and to all the churches to them committed.*

The king shall answer *With good will and devowt sowle I promit, and perfectly graunte, that to yow and euery of yow and all the churches to yow committed, I shall keepe the privileges of Lawe Canon and of the holie church, and dewe Lawe and rightfulnes. And I shall in asmoch as I may by reason and right, by gods grace defende yow, and euery of yow thoroughout my Realme, and all the churches to yow committed. All these thinges and euery of them I Henry king of Englande promit and confirme, so helpe me god, and by thes holie Evangelistes by me bodily towched vpon this holie aulter.*

And the king shall rise vpp of his Chaire, and by the Busshopps of Exceter and Ely shalbe ledde to the high Aulter, where he shall make a solempne othe vpon the same Aulter in the sight of all the people to observe all the premisses.

That done the Cardinall kneling, and the king lying groveling afore the high aulter as it is aboue the said Cardinall shall begynne w^t an high voyce the Imme *Veni creator Spiritus* et c. which Imme ended the same Cardinall shall say standing this oryson ouer the king: *Te Inuocamus.* and at the ende therof kneling agayne et c.

Immediately after which Oryson two busshops other two in the Quere shall begin and sing a Letany, and in the meane season the Cardinall w^t other busshops kneling shall say the seven psalmes and the said Letany till tyme the quere haue songe some of this oryson that enden *te Rogamus audi nos*, Among whome my Lorde Cardinall then standing at the high aulter shall sing w^t open voice three tymes, *vt presentem famulum tuum.* And at the ende thereof kneele againe till the quere haue done singing *Kyrie Eleyson.* And than shall he rise and saye. *Dominus vobiscum* w^t thes *Orysons Omnipotens Sempiterne Deus* et c. *Benedic Domine,* et c. *Deus ineffabilis,* et c. *Deus qui populis,* et c. At thende wherof when it is comen vnto thes wordes *per Omnia Secula Seculorum,* he shall chaunge his voice, and sing then in prelate wise vnto thes wordes. *Per Christum Dominum nostrum.* which wordes shalbe said in bace voice.

Thes orisons so being ended, the king that all this while hath Lyen groveling, shall rise and sit in the Chaire before the Cardinal, as was done before when the said Cardinall made certain Interrogacions, as, ye will keepe. In the wch Chaire after he hath somwhat rested himself he shall rise and go vp to the high aulter sustenid w^t the saide Busshops as aboue said, where as the king shalbe vnarayed and vnclothed by his chamberlain into his cote of Crymsen Satten largely openid as the shirte be, which all three cotes and ij shirtes shalbe openid afore and behinde on the shulders and the Elbowes by the said Cardinall, to thintent that in thes places he maye be anonynted.

And whiles he is anoynted Sr Thomas Montgomery, and Sr Thomas Burgh bene appointed for to holde a pall ouer him, and first the said Cardinall sitting, shall anoynte the king kneelyng w^t quisshins of holie oyle in the palmes of his bodie and his handes. Seying thes wordes. *Vngatur manus* w^t this collect *Respice ommipotens Deus* et c. The Quere singing in the meane tyme and contynually whiles the king is anoynting. *Vngerunt Regem* et c. and the Psalme. *Domine in virtute tua letabitur Rex,* et c. vntill he hath anoynted the king of the same oyle on his brestes in the middes of his back, on his twoo shulders, on his two elbowes and on his head w^t the said oyle making a crosse, and afterwarde making an other crosse w^t the holie creyme on his heade, after thende of the said Collect saying to euery place to be anoynted wordes convenyent, as in example to the heade thes wordes, *Vngatur Caput,* And to the shulders *Vngantur Scapule* et c. And it is to be remembred, that thabbot of westminster after the kinges anoynting, shall drye all the places of the bodie, where he was anoynted w^t some Coton or lynnen clothe, which is to be brent,[1] and furthw^t close and Lace again the openinges of the kinges said shirtes and cotes, putting on the kinges handes a paire of lynnen gloues to be brought thither by his said Chamberlain et c.

Then shall the said Cardinall say thes Orysons, *Deus Dei filius. et Deus qui es Justorum.*

This done the king shall rise, and also the Cardinall, the Abbot of westminster shall put on the king a Tabarde of Tartaryn white

---

[1] Burnt.

shapen in maner of a dalmatike, and he shall put on the kinges heade a Coyfe thesame to be Chamberleyn which shall continually abide vpon the kinges heade vntill the eight daye next following. At which daye after a solempne Masse said by a busshopp before the king, The said busshop shall take the coyfe from the kinges heade, and after the same wasshed, dryed, and kembed he shall put vpon it a Cyrcle of golde, the which he shall beare all that daye bareheaded in the reverence of his dealbacion.[1]

Sone after the said Cardinall shall blesse such ornamentes royall as followed, Singing the orison. *Deus Rex, Regina* et c. And the said Abbot shall put the same vpon the king, that is to say, a long cote vnto the heeles wrought before and behinde w^t great Images of golde, his hosen Saddles and spurres to be made meete for his legges and for his feete. Wherfore it is to be provided by the Sexten of westminster that all ornamentes royall w^t the Crowne be Layed vpon the high aulter before the kinges comyng, that all thinges maye be done w^t out Let.

After this his swearde shalbe blessed of the Cardinall saying this oryson. *Exaudi Domine preces nostras* et c which orison ended all the busshops shall deliver to him and sease him standing w^t a swearde, thei all Leying their handes on the same. And the Cardinall saying vnto him *Accipe gladium* et c. and w^t the same swearde shall girde himself.

The king thus girded w^t this swearde, and standing shall take Armyll of the Cardinall seying thes wordes. *Accipe Armula*. And it is to wit that Armyll in made is maner of a Stole woven w^t golde, and set w^t stones, to be put by the Cardinall about the kinges neck, and comyng from bothe shulders to his bothe elbowes, where thei shalbe fastenid by the abbot of westminster w^t Lace of silke to euery side the elbowe in two places, y^t is to say aboue thelbowes, and beneth. And at the same tyme the same cardinall shall set vpon the king aPall royall iiij square wouen all w^t golden Egles, the said Cardinall saying *Accipe Pallium*.

Herupon the Cardinall shall blesse the Crowne of Saynt Edward set on the high aulter saying this orison *Deus tuorum*. And first casting holie water, and saying the same shall set the Crowne vpon the kinges heade then sitting in his chaire before the high aulter. The saide Cardinall saying thes words. *Coronet te Deus* et c. W^t this orison *Deus perpetuitatis*. And there the quere shall sing this Antitheme. *Deus confortare, et esto vir* et c. w^t this psalme *Deus*

[1] Sacring.

regit me et c. Consequently the said Cardinall shall blesse a Ring w^t a Rubye, called the Regall for the king to be set on his iiij finge of the right hande w^t these orisons *Accipio Regno dignitatis* et c et *Deus cuius* et c.

Then the king shall take the swearde, wherw^t he was girde and offer it himself to god and to the aulter, and so shall take it agayn at the high aulter in token that his strenght and power should first come from god and holie churche. And the forsaid Swearde he shall deliver to some great Erle surely the same to be redemyd by the said Erle of thabbot for an hundreth shillinges, the which Erle shall after beare the said sweard naked before the king.

After this the Cardinall shall geve vnto the king in his right hande his Sceptre of gold w^t the dove on the toppe, the king hauing first put on his handes royall gloues by the said Cardinall saying in this wise. *Accipe Sceptrum,* w^t this orison *Omnium Domine Sanctis bonorum* et c. And the said cardinall shall deliuer to the king in his left hande the golden rodde w^t the crosse in the toppe saying in this wise. *Accipe virgam* et c. Blessing the king kneeling w^t this orison *Benedicat te Deus* et c.

The king thus by the Cardinall crowned w^t St Edwards crown, and by the Abbot arayed w^t Regall Sandalls and spurres, shalbe set agayn in his chaire before the high aulter where all the busshops on after an other shall come and kisse him. which so done the said Cardinall, all the busshops and other Lordes shall bring the king susteynid as aboue to the pulpit setting him in his Siege royall the said Cardinall begymnyng *Te Deum laudamus.* which ended the said Cardinall shall saye vnto the king *Sta, et retine amodo locum* et c.

The king to sit in his Siege roiall accompanied w^t all the Peres of the Realme, all the said Peeres to him shall make fealtie and homage vnder such wordes and fourme as followeth. Tharchbusshopps and busshops vnder this fourme. *Ye shall sweare that ye shalbe feathfull and trewe, and trowth and faith beare vnto the king our Soueraign Lorde, and to his heires kinges of England, And trewly ye shall do, and trewly knowledg the service dewe of the Landes the which ye claym to holde of him as in the right of your church As god shall helpe yow, and all holie Sayncts.*

And all the temporall Lordes vnder this fourme. *I become your Liegeman of Lief and Lymme, and of cathelic wo^rshipp, and faith and trowth shall beare vnto yow to Lyve and dye w^t yow against all maner folke, so god me helpe* et c.

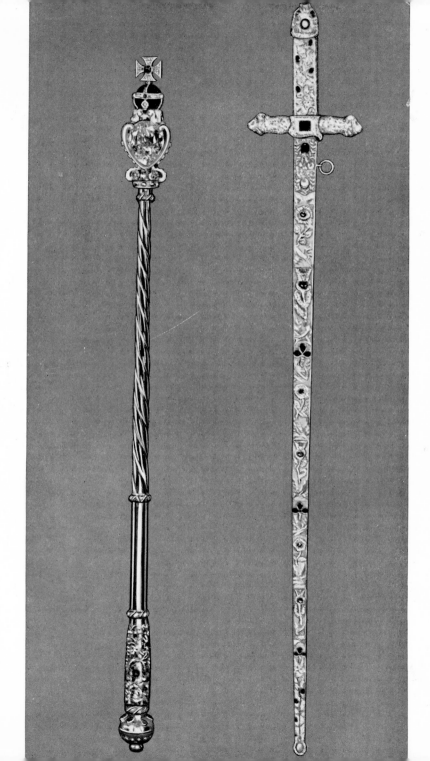

St. Edward's Crown; the Orb; the Sceptre with Cross; the Sceptre with Dove; the Rir
The Ampulla and the Spoon

That done, thei all holding vp their handes in tokenyng of their fidelitie shall offre themselfes to susteine, defende, and support the king, and his crown. And for easing of the king and his Laboures if nede be the said busshops of Exceter and Elye may set their handes to the crown in helping him to beare thesame. And in Likewise two of the greatest Lordes of his blood bearing the Sceptre and the Rodde.

Then the Queene as aboue shall go to the high aulter the greeces afore honorably arayed w^t carpettes and quisshions by the vsshers of his chambre, whervpon the Queene shall Lye prostrate, as the king did before. The cardinall saying ouer her this orison. *Deus qui solus habes.* et c. That ended she shall arise, and kneele, and by her the great Ladie, that shalbe alwayes attending vpon her. the Circle of golde taken from her head, and her breast by the cardinall openid, the same cardinall shall anoynt her two tymes first in the fore part of the head w^t holie oyle making a cross saying thes wordes. *In nomine patris et filij et spiritus sancti. Amen. Proficiat tibi hec vnctio.* Secondly w^t the same oyle in her brest. And the cardinall shall saye this orison. *Omnipotens sempiterne Deus* et c. which ended the said great Ladie shall close her breast. The cardinall after that shall blesse a riche Ring, saying this orison. *Creator* et c. Casting holiewater vpon it, and put the same Ring on the fourth finger of the Queenes right hande, saying in this wise. *Accipe annulum* et c. That ended, he shall say, *Dominus voiscum* w^t this collect, *Deus cuius* et c. After that the cardinall shall blesse the Queenes Crowne, saying. *Oremus, Deus tuorum.* Then he shall set the same crowne on the queenes head, having then a coyfe put theron by the great Ladie for conservacion of the holie vnction, which is afterward to be deliueryd to the said cardinall saying this orison. *Officio nostre* et c. He shall also deliuer vnto the queene a Sceptre in her right hande, and a rodde of golde in her left hande saying this orison. *Omnium domine.* et c.

The Queene thus crowned shalbe led by the aboue saied busshops of Exceter and Ely vnto her Siege of Estate nere the kinges Siege, making her obeisaunce afore the kinges Matie in her comyng therunto, the noble Ladies following her, and especially the great Ladie as is aboue being vnto her for her informacion and comfort. And in the same Siege the queene shall sit till the offitory be songe.

All the premisses dewly done, the office of the Masse that beginneth, *Protector noster,* shalbe begone of the rulers of the Quere, w^t the *Kyrie,* and *gloria in excelsis,* in what soeuer tyme the coronacion be, this orison *Omnipotens sempiterne deus* et c. And the *Epistle Charissimi*, the *Grayle, Dirigatur, alias Deus in cuius virtute*. The gospell. *Abeuntes*. And so furth the gospell being red the busshop of greatest estate, while the queere singeth the Crede shall beare the boke of the gospell to the king and to the Queene to kysse. And afterward to deliuer it to the Gospeller to beare the same to the Cardinall singing Masse. the said Crede being ended the rulers of the quere shall begine the offitory, *Intende voci*. And while that is in singing, the king crowned shalbe Ledde as aboue from his Siege royall to the pulpyt to the high aulter, his four sweardes all naked, his Sceptre, and his rod of golde borne before him as it is aforesaide. The Quene following in such estate as aboue to the cardinall having his face towarde the quere as is at the observaunce and offering accustomed the king shall offre an obley[1] of brede Layed vpon the Patene of S^t. Edwards chalice, w^t the which obley after consecrate the king shalbe howselled.[2] And aswell the said patene w^t the obley, as the Cruet w^t wyne shalbe deliuerid to him by the gospeller at tyme of his offering. The king also shall offree a marke in golde, and xvj^li. in coyne to him to be deliuerid by the said Chamberlayn. And the king kneeling and bowing his head, the Cardinall shall blesse him, saying ouer him thes orisons. *Omnipotens Sempiterne Deus*. et cet. *Benedic Domine* et c. Aftre the king the queene shall offree her offering as is accustomed.

This done the king and the Queene in forme as thei came shalbe brought to the Sieges royall and of estate, there to sit till *Agnus dei* be begon. The Secrete of the Masse *Munera domine*, The preface *Qui es fons* et c. The masse this wise to be said vnto the tyme the Cardinall haue songe the wordes. *Per omnia secula seculorum*, next *Agnus dei* which songen the cardinall pontifically arayed shall to^rne him to the king and the people blessing them w^t this orison. *omnipotens deus charismatum*, that ended, and the quere answering Amen. *Agnus dei* shalbe songe, and whiles the said quere is so singing, the chief busshop that afore bare the gospell booke to the king and the queene, shall beare the paxe[3] vnto them sitting in their Sieges royall of estate, and when the king and the queene haue kissed at the (paxe) thei shall descende, and be susteyned and accompanied as aboue, thei shall go vnto the high aulter, And after the Cardinall hath communicate himself, he having betwixt his handes the same Chalice, whervpon the holie

---

[1] Oblation. [2] Receive the Sacrament.
[3] Small disc of metal kissed in token of peace.

sacrament shalbe Leyd, shall toᵣne himself to the king and the queene. And thei lying prostrate before him shall say their *Confiteor*, all the prelates answering *Misereatur*, and the Cardinall saying *Absolutio*. That done the king and the queene shall somwhat arise kneeling, and wᵗ a great devocion receive the sacrament by the handes of the said Cardinall, two of the greatest busshops then present holding before the king and the queene a Long Towell of silke. This so done the king and the queene shall stande vp, and take wyne of the forseide Chalice by the handes of thabbot of westminster. All thes thing*es* reverently accomplished the king and the queene in maner and forme as thei came shall retoᵣne to their Sieges royall and of estate in the said pulpit. When thei be set the rulers of the quere shall begynne the *Postcommen Intelligite*. The cardinall singing this collect, *Presta quesumus*. And so ended the Mas.

The masse thus ended, the king accompanyed wᵗ the prelates and nobles, the Queene following him in ordre as aboue descende from their Sieges royall and of estate, and go to the high aulter, where the cardinall being in a pontificall araye as he sange Masse wᵗ all the other the said prelates and Lordes following. And there the cardinall shall take the crowne of the king and queenes heads and set them on the awlter.

And it is to wit that a certain place nere the said Shryne must be preparate wᵗ trauers and curtens by the vshers of the kinges chambre, wherto the king immediately shall go and there breake his fast if himself List And there also the said chamberlayn shall take for the king all the Regalls aforesaid, and peace by peace deliuer them to the Abbot of westminster, the same by him to be Layed vpon the said Awlter. And the king thus vnarayed by the sayd chamberlayn of his Regalls to his cote and shirte, shalbe by the said Chamberlayn newe arayed wᵗ hosen Sandalls and other robes of estate, that is to saye, a Syrcote of purple veluet close or openid furred wᵗ golde and the colloᵣ, handes,[1] and wpeyres,[2] and hoode of estate furred wᵗ Ermyns powdred and purfellid wᵗ a great lace of silk, and two tarsells purple. And the king at his pleasure may weare mo of his robes vnder his mantell as a Tabarde, a kyrtle or any of them. For the queene also shalbe ordeynid an other closet nere to the Awlter, where shalbe chaunged by her gentle-women of her chambre into newe garmentes, viz a Circle royall of purple veluet, a Mantell wᵗ a Trayne of the same.

[1] Cuffs.   [2] Uppers.

The king by his Chamberlayne, and the Queene by her gentle-women thus of newe in their robes arayed, shall go from their closettes to the said Awlter afore the Shryne of S^t. Edward where the said Cardinall in Pontificalibus as at Masse, shall put vpon their heades two other crownes meete for the same. And the king and the queene having in their handes their Sceptres, shall go from the said Shrine by the great awlter to the said pulpit, where at their pleasure thei may sit in their Sieges roiall and of estate and talke w^t their Lordes temporall vnto such tyme as the said cardinall and prelates may put them in other robes.

And as for the order of the kinges reto^{r}ning from Westminster church to his pallaice. First the king in his robes of estate susteinid by busshops as aboue in their robes, And the Chamberlayn bearing his trayne shall go in great triumphe vnder the Cele borne by the v. portes as aboue from the Pulpit by the same way as he came his rodde, and foure sweardes borne by the same estates as afore, whereof two of them, y^t is to say, Curtana, and the sweard that he was girde w^t both flatt w^t out sharpe poyntes shalbe borne naked. The other two in Scabardes in tokening that a king ought more to remembre man than straitnesse of Judgement. The cardinall, all Lordes Spirituall in their robes, the great officers, and all other Lordes temporall also in their robes and set in dewe order as aboue said w^t the knightes of the Bathe, and other noblemen, w^t harawldes officers of Armes, trumpettes and Mynstrells shall attende vpon him throughout Westminster hall. When he hath at his pleasure somewhat rested him in the same estate w^t thes nobles, he may reto^{r}ne into the said hall there royally to be seruid as is according to the feast of his Coronacion etc.

APPENDIX A
(ii)

JOHN EVELYN AND SAMUEL PEPYS AT THE CORONATION OF KING CHARLES II

Save for the joy of the people at their liberation from the tyranny of Cromwell, his Major-Generals and the Puritans there was little unusual in the coronation of Charles II. The ancient Regalia of England which had been defaced and smashed under the Commonwealth had to be replaced and some account of this has been given in Chapter 6 (The Regalia). However, two lively and accomplished reporters were present and they must be allowed to tell their tales in their own way.

John Evelyn reported:

> The coronation of His Majesty Charles II was in the Abby Church of Westminster, at all which ceremonie I was present. The King and all his Nobility went to the Tower, I accompanying my Lord Viscount Mordaunt part of the way; this was on Sunday the 22nd, but indeed his Majestie went not til early this morning, and proceeded from thence to Westminster in this order:

> First went the Duke of York's Horse Guards, Messengers of the Chamber, 136 Esquires to the Knights of the Bath, each of whom had two, most richly habited. The Knight Harbinger. Sergeant Porter. Sewers of the Chamber. Quarter Waiters. Six Clearks of Chancery. Clearke to the Signet. Clearke of the Privy Seale. Clearks of the Council, of the Parliament, and of the Crowne. Chaplaines in ordinary having dignitaries 10. Kings Advocats and Remembrancer. Council at Law. Members of the Chancery. Puisne Sergeants. King's Attorney and Solicitor. King's eldest Sergeant. Secretaries of the French and Latine tongue. Gent Ushers, Daily Waiters, Sewers, Carvers, and Cup-bearers in ordinary. Esquires of the Body 4. Masters of standing Offices being no Councellors, viz: – of the Tents, Revels, Ceremonies, Armorie, Wardrobe, Ordnance, Requests. Chamberlaine of the Exchequer. Barons of the Exchequer. Judges. Lord Chiefe Baron. Lord C. Justice of the Common Pleas. Master of the Rolls. Lord C. Justice of England. Trumpets. Gentlemen of the Privy Chamber. Knights of the Bath, 68, in crimson robes exceeding rich and the noblest shew of the whole cavalcade, His Majestie excepted. Knt. Marshall. Treasurer of the Chamber. Master of the Jewells. Lord of the Privy Council. Comptroller of the Household. Treasurer of the Household. Trumpets. Sergeant Trumpet. Two Pursuivants-at-Armes. Barons. Two Pursuivants-of-Armes. Viscounts, Two Heraulds. Earles. Lord Chamberlaine of the Household. Two Heraulds. Marquisses. Dukes. Heralds

Clarencieux and Norroy. Lord Chancellor. Lord High Steward of England. Two persons representing the Dukes of Normandy and Aquitaine, viz: – Sir Richard Fanshawe and Sir Herbert Price in fantastic habits of the time. Gentlemen Ushers. Garter. Lord Maior of London. The Duke of York alone (the rest by two's). Lord High Constable of England. Lord Great Chamberlaine, of England. The Sworde borne by the Earle Marshal of England. The King in royal robes and equipage. Afterwarde follow'd Equerries, Footemen Gent Pensioners. Master of the Horse leading a horse richly caprison'd. Vice Chamberlaine. Captain of the Pensioners. Captain of the Guard. The Guard. The Horse Guard. The Troope of Volunteers with many other Officers and Gentlemen. This magnificent traine on horseback, as rich as embroidery, velvet, cloth of gold and silver, and jewells, could make them and their prancing horses, proceed'd thro' the streetes shrew'd with flowers, houses hung with rich tapessry, windowes and balconies full of ladies; the London Militia lining the ways, and the severall Companies with their banners and loud musiq rank'd in their orders; the fountaines running wine, belle ringing, with speeches made at the severall triumphal arches; at that of the Temple Barr (neere which I stood) the Lord Maior was receiv'd by the Bayliff of Westminster, who, in a scarlet robe, made a speech. Thence with joyful acclamation his Majestie passed to Whitehall. Bonfires at night.

The next day, being St George's, he went by water to Westminster Abby. When his Majestie was enter'd, the Deane and Prebendaries brought all the regalia and deliver'd them to severall Noblemen to beare before the King, who met them at the west doore of the Church singing an anthem, to the Quire. Then came the Peers in their robes, and coronets in their hands, til his Majestie was plac'd in a throne elevated before the altar. Then the Bishop of London (the Archbishop of Canterbury being sick) went to every side of the throne to present the King to the people, asking if they would have him for their King and do him homage; at this they shouted 4 times GOD SAVE KING CHARLES THE SECOND! Then an anthem was sung. Then his Majestie attended by 3 Bishops went up to the altar, and he offer'd a pall and a pound of gold. Afterwards he sate downe in another chaire during the sermon, which was preach'd by Dr Morley then Bishop of Worcester. After sermon the King took his oath before the altar to maintain the Religion, Magna Charta, and Laws of the Land. The hymn Veni S. Sp. follow'd, and then the Litany by 2 Bishops. Then the Archbishop of Canterbury, present but much indispos'd and weake, said LIFT UP YOUR HEARTS; at which the King rose up and put off his robes and upper garments, and was in a waistcote so opened in divers places that the Archb'p might commodiously anoint him, first in the palmes of his hands, when an anthem was sung and a prayer read; then his breast and betwixt the shoulders, bending of both armes, and lastly on the crowne of the head, with apposite hymns and prayers at each anoynting; this don, the Deane clos'd and button'd up the waistcoate. Then was a coyfe put on, and the cobbium, syndon, or dalmatic, and over this a supertunic of cloth of gold, with buskins and sandals of the same, spurrs, and the sword, a prayer being first said over it by the Lord Chamberlaine. Then the armill, mantle, etc. Then the Archbishop plac'd the crowne imperial on the altar, pray'd over it, and set it on his Majestie's head, at which all the Peers put on their coronets. Anthems and rare musiq, with lutes, viols, trumpets, organs, and voices, were then heard, and the Archbishop put a ring on his Majestie's finger. The King next offer'd his sword on the altar, which being redeemed was drawn and borne before him. Then the Archbishop deliver'd him the sceptre with the dove in one hand, and in the other the sceptre with the globe.[1] Then the King kneeling, the Archbishop pronounc'd the blessing. The King then ascending againe his Royal Throne, whilst Te Deum was singing, all the Peers did their homage, by every one touching his crowne. The Archbishop and the rest of the Bishops first kissing the King; who receiv'd the holy sacrament, and so disrob'd, yet with the imperial crowne on his head and accompanied with all the Nobility in the former order, he went on foote upon blew cloth, which was spread and reach'd from the West dore of the Abby to Westminster stayres, when he took water in a triumphal barge to Whitehall, where was extraordinary feasting.[2]

Samuel Pepys was also there:—

CORONATION DAY, 1661.

About four I rose and got to the Abbey, where I followed Sir J. Denham, the surveyor, with some company he was leading in. And with much ado, by the favour of Mr Cooper, his man, did get up into a great scaffold across the north end of the Abbey, where with a great deal of patience I sat from past four till eleven before the King came in. And a great pleasure it was to see the Abbey raised in the middle, all covered with red, and a throne (that is, a chair) and footstool on the top of it; and all the officers of all kinds so much as the very fiddlers in red vests. At last comes in the Dean and Prebendaries of Westminster, with the Bishops (many of them in cloth of gold copes), and after them the Nobility, all in their Parliament robes, which was a most magnificent sight. Then the Duke and the King with a sceptre (carried by my Lord Sandwich) and sword and mond (orb) before him, and the crown too. The King in his robes, bareheaded which was very fine. And after all had placed themselves, there was a sermon and a service; and then in the Choir at the high altar the King passed through all the ceremonies of the Coronation, which to my great grief I and most in the Abbey could not see. The crown being put upon his head, a great shout began, and he came forth to the throne, and there passed through more ceremonies; as taking the oath, and having things read to him by the Bishop; and his lords who put on their caps as soon as the King put on his crown and came, and kneeled before him. And three times the King-at-Arms went to the open places on the scaffold, and proclaimed, that

[1] This is a mistake. It must have been the sceptre with the cross.
[2] Evelyn is wrong again. The banquet was, as usual, in Westminster Hall.

if any one could show any reason why Charles Stewart should not be King of England, that now he should come and speak. And a General Pardon also was read by the Lord Chancellor, and medals flung up and down by my Lord Cornwallis, of silver, but I could not come by any. But so great a noise that I could make but little of the music; and indeed, it was lost to everybody. I went out a little while before the King had done all his ceremonies, and went round the Abbey to West-minster Hall, all the way within rails, and 10,000 people, with the ground covered with blue cloth; and scaffolds all the way. Into the Hall I got, where it was very fine with hangings and scaffolds one upon another, full of brave ladies; and my wife in one little one, on the right hand. Here I stayed walking up and down, and at last upon one of the side stalls I stood and saw the King come in with all the persons (but the soldiers) that were yesterday in the cavalcade; and a most pleasant sight it was to see them in their several robes.

And the King came in with his crown on, and his sceptre in his hand, under a canopy borne up by six silver staves, carried by Barons of the Cinque Ports and little bells at every end. And after a long time he got up to the farther end, and all set themselves down at their several tables; and that was also a brave sight; and the King's first course carried up by the Knights of the Bath. And many fine ceremonies there was of the Herald's leading up goodly people before him, and bowing; and my Lord of Albermarle's going to the kitchen and eating a bit of the first dish that was to go to the King's table. But, above all, was these three Lords, Northumberland, and Suffolk, and the Duke of Ormond, coming before the courses on horseback, and staying so all dinner-time, and at last bringing up (Dymock) the King's Champion, all in armour on horseback, with his spear and target carried before him. And a Herald proclaims 'That if any dare deny Charles Stewart to be lawful King of England, here was a Champion that would fight with him'; and with these words, the Champion flings down his gauntlet, and all this he does three times in his going up towards the King's table. At last, when he is come, the King drinks to him, and then sends him the cup, which is of gold, and he drinks it off, and then rides back again with the cup in his hand. I went from table to table to see the Bishops and all others at their dinner, and was infinitely pleased with it. And at the Lords' table I met with William Howe, and he spoke to my Lord for me, and he did give him four rabbits and a pullet, and so Mr Creed and I got Mr Minshell to give us some bread, and so we at a stall ate it, as everybody else did what they could get. I took a great deal of pleasure to go up and down, and look upon the ladies, and to hear the music of all sorts, but above all the 24 violins. About six at night they had dined, and I went up to my wife. And strange it is to think that these two days have held up fair till now that all is done, and the King gone out of the Hall; and then it fell a-raining and thundering and lightning as I have not seen it do for some years; which people did take great notice of; God's blessing of the work of these two days, which is a foolery to take too much notice of such things. I observed little disorder in all this, only the King's footmen had got hold of the canopy, and would keep it from the Barons of the Cinque Ports.

Sometimes the amateur scoops the professional reporter, at least in some part of the story, and Bishop Kennett has left a fuller account than Pepys of this imbroglio:

No sooner had the aforesaid Barons brought up the King to the foot of the stairs in Westminster Hall ascending to his throne, and turned on the left hand (toward their own table) out of the way but the King's footmen most insolently and violently seized the canopy, which the Barons endeavouring to keep and defend, were by their number and strength dragged down to the lower end of the Hall, nevertheless still keeping their hold; and had not Mr Owen, York Herald, being accidently near the Hall door, and seeing the contest, caused the same to be shut, the footmen had certainly carried it away by force. But in the interim also (speedy notice hereof having been given to the King) one of the Querries was sent from him, with command to imprison the footmen, and dismiss them out of his service, which put an end to the present disturbance. These footmen were also commanded to make their submission to the Court of Claims, which was accordingly done by them the 30th April following, and the canopy then delivered back to the said Barons.

APPENDIX A

(iii)

JAMES HEMING AND HORACE WALPOLE AT THE CORONATION OF KING GEORGE III

A full account of the coronation of George III is to be found in a letter by Mr James Heming published in the Annual Register for 1761.

'As the friendship of Mr. Rolles, who had procured me a pass-ticket, as they call it, enabled me to be present both in the hall and the abbey; and as I had a fine view of the procession out of doors, from a one pair of stairs room, which your neighbour, Sir Edward, had hired at the small price of one hundred guineas, on purpose to oblige his acquaintance, I will endeavour to give you as minute an account as I can of all the particulars omitted in the public papers. First then, conceive to yourself the fronts of the houses in all the streets, that could command the least point of view, lined with scaffolding, like so many galleries or boxes, raised one above another to the very roofs. These were covered with carpets and cloths of different colours, which presented a pleasant variety to the eye; and if you consider the brilliant appearance of the spectators who were seated in them (many being richly drest), you will easily imagine that this was no indifferent part of the show. The mob underneath made a pretty contrast to the rest of the company. Add to this, that though we had nothing but wet and cloudy weather for some time before, the day cleared up, and the sun shone auspiciously, as it were in compliment to the grand festival. Had it rained half the spectators were so exalted that they could not have seen the ceremony, as a temporary roof put over the platform, on account of the uncertainty of the weather, was exceeding low. This roof was covered with a kind of sail-cloth; which on orders being given to roll it up, an honest Jack Tar climbed up to the top, and stripped it off in a minute or two; whereas the persons appointed for that service might have been an hour about it. This gave us not only a more extensive view, but let the light in on every part of the procession. I should tell you, that a rank of foot soldiers were placed on each side within the platform; which was an encroachment on the spectators; for at the last coronation I am informed they stood below it; and it was not a little surprising to see the officers familiarly conversing and walking arm-in-arm with many of them till we were let into the secret, that they were gentlemen who had put on the dresses of common soldiers for what purpose I need not mention. On the outside were stationed, at proper distances, several parties of horse-guards, whose horses somewhat incommoded the people, that pressed incessantly upon them, by their prancing and capering; though luckily I do not hear of any great mischief being done. I must confess it gave me pain to see the soldiers, both horse and foot, obliged most unmercifully to belabour the heads of the mob with their broad swords, bayonets, and musquets; but it was not unpleasant to observe several tipping the horse soldiers slily from time to time (some with halfpence and some with silver as they could muster up the cash); to let them pass between the horses to get nearer the platform; after which these unconscionable gentry drove them back again. As soon as it was day-break (for I chose to go to my place over-night), we were diverted with seeing the coaches and chairs of the nobility and gentry passing along with much ado; and several persons, very richly drest, were obliged to quit their equipages and be escorted by the soldiers through the mob to their respective places. Several carriages I am told received great damage; Mr. Jennings whom you know, had his chariot broke to pieces, but providentially neither he nor Mrs. Jennings who were in it, received any hurt.

'My pass-ticket would have been of no service, if I had not prevailed on one of the guards, by the irresistible argument of half a crown, to make way for me through the mob to the hall-gate, where I got admittance just as their Majesties were seated at the upper end, under magnificent canopies.

'There seemed to be no small confusion in marshalling the ranks, which is not to be wondered at, considering the length of the cavalcade, and the numbers that were to walk. At length, however, everything was regularly adjusted, and the procession began to quit the hall between eleven and twelve. The platform leading to the west door of the abbey, was covered with blue cloth for the train to walk on; but there seemed to be a defect in not covering the upright posts that supported the awning, as it is called, which looked mean and naked, with that or some other coloured cloth. The nobility walked two by two. Being willing to see the procession pass along the platform through the streets, I hastened from the hall, and by the assistance of a soldier, made my way to my former station at the corner of Bridge Street where the windows commanded a double view at the turning. I shall not attempt to describe the splendour and magnificence of the whole; and words must fall short of that innate joy and satisfaction which the spectators felt and expressed, especially as their Majesties passed by; on whose countenance a dignity suited to their station, tempered with the most amiable complacency, was sensibly impressed. It was observable that as their Majesties and the nobility passed the corner which commanded a prospect of Westminster Bridge, they stopped short, and turned back to look at the people, whose appearance as they had their hats off, and were thick-planted on the ground, which rose gradually, I can compare to nothing but a pavement of heads and faces.

'I had the misfortune not to be able to get to the abbey time enough to see all that passed there; nor, indeed, when I got in, could I have so distinct a view as I could have wished. But our friend Harry Whitaker had the luck to be stationed in the first row of the gallery behind the seats allotted for the nobility, close to the square platform, which was erected by the altar, with an ascent of three steps for their Majesties to be crowned on. You are obliged to him, therefore, for several particulars which I could not otherwise had informed you of. The sermon, he tells me, lasted only fifteen minutes. The King was anointed on the crown of his head, his breast, and the palmes of his hands. At the very instant the crown was placed on the King's head, a fellow, having been placed on the top of the abbey-dome, from whence he could look down into the chancel, with a flag which he dropt as a signal, the park and Tower guns began to fire, the trumpets sounded, and the Abbey echoed with the repeated shouts and acclamations of the people; which, on account of the aweful silence, that had hitherto reigned had a very striking effect. As there were no commoners knights of the garter; instead of caps and vestments peculiar to the order, they being all peers, wore the robes and coronets of their respective ranks. When the queen had received the scepter with the cross, and the ivory rod with the dove, her Majesty was conducted to a magnificent throne on the left hand of his Majesty.

'I cannot but lament that I was not near enough to observe their Majesties performing the most serious and solemn acts of devotion; but I am told, that the reverent attention which both paid, when (after having made their second oblations) the next ceremony was their receiving the holy communion, it brought to the mind of every one near them, a proper recollection of the consecrated place in which they were.

'An hour lost in the morning is not so easily recovered. This was the case in the present instance; for to whatever it might be owing, the procession most assuredly set off too late; besides, according to what Harry observed, there were such long pauses between some of the ceremonies in the abbey, as plainly shewed all the actors were not perfect in their parts. However it be, it is impossible to conceive the chagrin and disappointment, which the late return of the procession occasioned; it being so late indeed, that the spectators, even in the open air had but a very dim and gloomy view of it, while to those who sat patiently in Westminster Hall, waiting its return for six hours, scarce a glimpse of it appeared as the branches were not lighted till just upon his Majesty's entrance. I had flattered myself, that a new scene of splendid grandeur would have been presented to us in the return of the procession from the reflection of the lights, &c., and had posted back to the hall with all possible expedition; but I was greatly disappointed. The whole was confusion, irregularity and disorder.

'However, we were afterwards amply recompensed for this partial eclipse, by the bright picture which the lighting of the chandeliers presented to us. Conceive to yourself if you can conceive what I own I am at a loss to describe, so magnificent a building as that of Westminster Hall, lighted up with near three thousand wax candles in most splendid branches, our crowned heads, and almost the whole nobility, with the prime of our gentry, most superbly arrayed, and adorned with a profusion of the most brilliant jewels, and galleries on every side crowded with company, for the most part elegantly and richly dressed; – but to conceive it in all its lustre, I am conscious it is absolutely necessary to have been present. To proceed with my narration. – Their Majesties table was served with three courses, at the first of which Earl Talbot as steward of his Majesty's household, rode up from the hall gate to the steps leading to where their Majesties sat, and on his returning the spectators were presented with an unexpected sight in his lordship's backing his horse, that he might keep his face still towards the King. A loud clapping and huzzaing consequently ensued.

'After the first course and before the second, the king's champion, Mr. Dymocke, who enjoys that office as being lord of the manor of Scrivelsby in Lincolnshire, entered the hall, completely armed, in one of his Majesty's best suits of white armour, mounted on a fine white horse, the same his late Majesty rode at the battle of Dettingen, richly caparisoned, in the following manner:

'Two trumpets, with the champion's arms on their banners; the serjeant trumpet with his mace on his shoulder; the champion's two esquires, richly habited, one on the right hand with the champion's lance carried upright; the other on the left hand, with his target, and the champion's arms depicted thereon; the herald of arms with a paper in his hand, containing the words of the challenge.

'The earl marshall in his robes and coronet, on horseback, with the marshall's staff in his hand: the champion on horseback, with a gauntlet in his right hand, his helmet on his head adorned with a great plume of feathers, white, blue, and red: the lord high constable in his robes and coronet, and collar of the order, on horseback, with the constable's staff.

'Four pages richly apparelled, attendants on the champion.

'The passage to their Majesties table being cleared by the knights marshall, the herald at arms, with a loud voice, proclaimed the champion's challenge, at the lower end of the hall, in the words following:

' "If any person, of what degree soever, high or low, shall deny or gainsay, Our Sovereign Lord King George III, king of Great Britain, France, and Ireland, defender of the faith &c., (grandson) and next heir to sovereign lord king (George II.) the last king deceased, to be the right heir to the imperial crown of the realm of Great Britain, or that he ought not to enjoy the same; here is his champion who saith that he lyeth, and is a false traitor being ready in person to combat with him; and in this quarrel will adventure his life against him, on what day soever shall be appointed."

'And then the champion throws down his gauntlet; which, having lain some small time, the herald took up and returned it to the champion.

'Then they advanced in the same order to the middle of the hall, where the said herald made proclamation as before; and lastly to the foot of the steps, when the said herald, and those who preceded him, going to the top of the steps, made proclamation a third time, at the end whereof the champion cast down his gauntlet, which after some time being taken up, and returned to him by the herald, he made a low obeisance to his Majesty; whereupon the cupbearer, assisted as before, brought to the King a gilt bowl of wine, with a cover; his Majesty drank to the champion, and sent him the said bowl by the cupbearer, accompanied with his assistants; which the champion (having put on his gauntlet) received, and retiring a little drank thereof, and made his humble reverence to his Majesty; and being accompanied as before, rode out of the hall taking the said bowl and cover with him as his fee.

'You cannot expect that I should give you a bill of fare, or enumerate the dishes that were provided and sent from the adjacent temporary kitchens, erected in Cotton Garden for this purpose. No less than sixty haunches of venison, with a surprising quality of all sort of game, were laid in for this grand feast. The King's table was covered with 120 dishes at three several times, served up by his Majesty's band of pensioners; but what chiefly attracted our eyes was their Majesties desert, in which the confectioner had lavished all his ingenuity in rock work and emblematical figures. The other deserts were no less admirable for their expressive devices.

'But I must not forget to tell you, that when the company came to be seated the poor Knights of the Bath had been overlooked, and no table provided for them. An airy apology, however, was served up to them instead of a substantial dinner; but the two junior knights in order to preserve their rank of precedency to their successors, were placed at the head of the judges table above all the learned brethren of the coif. The peers were placed on the outermost side of the tables, and the peeresses within, nearest to the walls. You cannot suppose that there was the greatest order imaginable observed during dinner, but must conclude that some of the company were as eager and impatient to satisfy the craving of their appetites, as any of your country squires at a race or assize ordinary.

'It was pleasant to see the various stratagems made use of by the company in the galleries to come in for a smack of the good things below. The ladies clubbed their handkerchiefs together to draw up a chicken or a bottle of wine. Some had been so provident as to bring baskets with them, which were let down, like the prisoners boxes at Ludgate or the Gate house, with a Pray remember the poor.

'You will think it high time that I should bring this long letter to a conclusion. Let it suffice then to acquaint you, that their Majesties returned to St. James's a little after ten o'clock at night;

but they were pleased to give time for the peeresses to go first, that they might not be incommoded by the pressure of the mob to see their Majesties. After the nobility were departed, the hall doors were thrown open according to custom, when the people immediately cleared it of all the moveables, such as the victuals, cloths, plates, dishes, &c., and, in short, everything that could stick to their fingers.

'I need not tell you, that several coronation medals of silver were thrown among the populace at the return of the procession. One of them was pitched into Mrs. Dixon's lap, as she sat upon a scaffold in Palace-yard. Some of gold were also thrown among the peeresses within the Abbey, just after the King was crowned, but they thought it beneath their dignity to stoop to pick them up.

'Our friend Harry who was upon the scaffold, at the return of the procession, closed in with the rear; at the expense of half a guinea was admitted into the hall; got brimfull of his Majesty's claret; and in the universal plunder brought off the glass her Majesty drank in, which is placed in the beaufet as a valuable curiosity.

'I should not forget telling you that I am well assured the King's crown weighs almost three pounds and a half, and that the great diamond in it fell out in returning to Westminster Hall, but was immediately found and restored.

'My wife desires her compliments to you; she was greatly pleased with the sight. All friends are well except that little Nancy Green has got a swelled face by being up all night; and Tom Moffat has his leg laid up on a stool, on account of a broken shin, which he got by a kick from a trooper's horse as a reward for his mobbing it. I shall say nothing of the illuminations at night; the newspapers must have told you of them, and that the Admiralty in particular, was remarkably lighted up. I expect to have from you an account of the rejoicings at your little town; and desire to know whether you was able to get a slice of the ox, which was roasted whole on this occasion.

I am dear Sir,
Yours most heartily,
JAMES HEMING

'P.S. – The princess dowager of Wales, with the younger branches of the royal family, had a box to see the coronation in the abbey, and afterwards dined in an apartment by themselves adjoining the hall.'

Dr G. F. Fisher, Archbishop of Canterbury, with his Chaplain

Dr A. C. Don, Dean of Westminster, in the Coronation Robes he will wear at the Ceremony

That old gossip Horace Walpole found in the coronation of George III much material for letters to his friends. The following is an extract from a letter he wrote to the Honourable Henry Seymour Conway:—

'Arlington Street.   September 25 1761.

'The Coronation is over: 'tis even a more gorgeous sight than I imagined. I saw the procession and the Hall; but the return was in the dark. In the morning they had forgot the Sword of State, the chairs for King and Queen, and their canopies. They used the Lord Mayor's for the first, and made the last in the Hall: so they did not set forth till noon; and then, by a childish compliment to the King, reserved the illumination of the Hall till his entry; by which means they arrived like a funeral, nothing being discernible but the plumes of the Knights of the Bath, which seemed the hearse. Lady Kildare, the Duchess of Richmond, and Lady Pembroke were the capital beauties. Lady Harrington, the finest figure at a distance; old Westmoreland, the most majestic. Lady Hertford could not walk, and indeed I think is in a way to give us great anxiety. She is going to Ragley to ride. Lord Beauchamp was one of the King's train-bearers. Of all the incidents of the day, the most diverting was what happened to the Queen. She had a retiring-chamber, with *all* conveniences, prepared behind the altar. She went thither – in the *most convenient* what found she but – the Duke of Newcastle! Lady Hardwicke died three days before the ceremony, which kept away the whole house of Yorke. Some of the peeresses were dressed overnight, slept in armchairs, and were waked if they tumbled their heads. Your sister Harris's maid, Lady Peterborough, was a comely figure. My Lady Cowper refused, but was forced to walk with Lady Macclesfield. Lady Falmouth was not there; on which George Selwyn said, "that those peeresses who were most used to *walk*, did not." I carried my Lady Townshend, Lady Hertford, Lady Anne Connolly, my Lady Hervey, and Mrs. Clive, to my deputy's house at the gate of Westminster Hall. My Lady Townshend said she should be very glad to see a Coronation, as she never had seen one. "Why", said I, "Madam, you walked at the last?" "Yes, child", said she, "but I saw nothing of it: I only looked to see who looked at me." '

APPENDIX A
(iv)

'THE MIRROR'S' ACCOUNT OF THE CORONATION OF KING WILLIAM IV

IN WESTMINSTER ABBEY,
Thursday, September 8, 1831.

By the courtesy of Sir George Nayler, Garter King at Arms, we were favoured with the privilege of witnessing this sublime and splendid ceremony, which we shall proceed to describe as fully as our columns will admit. We must, however, be concise in many particulars, from our want of space, as well as from some of the details having already been before the public. Our aim is to condense the official accounts, collate those of our principal contemporaries, and compare them with our own notes, not forgetting several points in themselves of minor importance, but contributing to the completeness of the whole.

PREPARATIONS IN THE ABBEY

Accommodation was provided for 5,300 persons within the Abbey, and such were their stability and finish, that they had anything but the appearance of erections for a temporary purpose. These had occupied many previous weeks, and their economy of space, and elegance of effect could only be the result of much experience and deliberation.

From the great western door of the Abbey, on the outside, a covered way was constructed, extending about fifty feet, at the entrance of which their Majesties and suite were to alight. This entrance was constructed entirely of wood, but painted on the outside and in the interior – the exterior to resemble stone, in keeping with the architecture of the Abbey, and the sides and roof of the interior an admirable imitation of Gothic panelling in oak. There were two stained windows about midway in the porch, on the walls of which were emblazoned the national emblems in lozenges, shields, and other heraldic devices. Adjoining this portico were two robing-rooms, fitted with crimson and gold, and convenient ante-rooms. The external and internal finish of this building almost made one regret that it should be allowed but to stand a brief day.

On entering the nave, on each side were boxes fitted up by the Dean and Chapter, filling up the spaces between the columns, extending far back, amphitheatrically, and covered with crimson cloth. Galleries covered also with crimson cloth were suspended from the vaultings, the full extent of the nave. To these boxes and galleries alone could admission be obtained for money: they afforded only a view of the procession as it passed on to the choir, all view of the ceremony in the choir from hence being shut out by an addition to the beautiful Gothic screen, which separates the nave and the choir. This addition was of wood, yet painted so skilfully to harmonize with the rich work of the screen, as almost to baffle detection. This was executed by Mr. Parris, the celebrated painter of the Colosseum. High above the doorway, on one side appears, (for it is not yet removed,) the effigies of Edward the Confessor, who rebuilt the Abbey; and on the other side Henry III. who enlarged it: both of these figures are in niches, canopied. Above them, beneath the pinnacled cornice is a row of emblazoned shields. The whole is painted with great ability, and as a work of art, would have delighted even Capon, the famous architectural scene-painter. This raised screen encloses the organ and loft, which were occupied by musicians and choristers, under the direction of Sir George Smart, and it operated as a sort of sounding-board to the music, by aiding to confine the sound within the choir.

At the commencement of the choir there was an ascent of several steps, and again the same at the distance of a few yards, which placed the spectator on the 'theatre', where the splendid pageant was enacted. This 'theatre', as it is called, formed the floor of the 'House', which was constructed within the walls of this vast and venerable pile, and might more appropriately be called the 'pit', as it was the lowest part of the structure. The approach to the 'theatre' through the choir was between inclosed ranges of seats, set apart for the great officers of state, the judges, &c., and the household. In the centre of the 'theatre', opposite the altar, between the transepts, and of course immediately beneath the great lantern over the tower, was raised the platform upon which were placed the chairs of state, or thrones, for the King and Queen. These platforms were square; that for the Queen smaller than the King's, and ascended by only three steps, whereas the King's had five. The platforms, to the base of the first step, were covered with cloth of gold, and from thence to the flooring of the 'theatre', with rich Wilton carpet. The King's chair stood on the right, facing the altar. The distance from the platforms to the *sacrarium* in front of the altar, where the coronation chairs stood, was not more than eight or nine feet.

The north and south transepts were fitted up with rows of benches, and close to each window an extensive gallery was erected. The first ten rows of benches on each side were kept for the peers and peeresses – the peers sitting on the right, and the peeresses on the left of their Majesties' chairs of state. Above these rows were others preserved for persons admitted with peerage tickets. On each side of the transepts were large galleries, ornamented with great elegance, but, unfortunately, not filled.

The Sacrarium, called in the printed ceremonial the area, exceeded all the other preparations in magnificence of decoration.

The first object which attracted the eye was the altar. The table, 6 feet 9 inches in length, stood upon a platform a little above the elevation of the floor, and had a small shelf behind. The whole was covered with blue and gold brocade. The top of this covering was panelled with broad gold lace, and was edged with gold looped fringe. The bottom and sides were bordered with gold lace, and the whole was furnished with a gold fringe, 7 inches deep. On this were subsequently placed the articles necessary in the coronation.

The back of the altar was covered with blue and gold brocade * * *. This drapery was coiled up with ropes of gold. It was surmounted by a cornice composed of two-inch-and-a-half gold and silk rope, with large gilt rosettes to each pipe. The fringe was of gold and silk, four inches deep. On the left hand, or north side, of the altar stood the chair of the Archbishop of Canterbury; it was of oak. The back, seat, and elbows were stuffed and covered with velvet of the colour called bishops' purple, and were panelled with gold lace. There was a footstool to match, which was covered with purple velvet, and ornamented with gymp. Besides this, there was a kneeling cushion for the Archbishop, covered with purple velvet, and a similar cushion for the Dean of Westminster on the other side. The step leading to the altar and the floor of the sacrarium was covered with a rich garter blue and gold Wilton carpet. The pattern was the Norman rose with the ermine. On the right of the altar stood the offering-table, which was covered with garter blue Genoa velvet, bordered with lace, and fringed with gold. Upon this, preparatory to the ceremonies, was placed a cushion, upon which the offerings were to be made, covered with garter blue velvet, panelled with gold lace, and with four gold tassels at the corners. The whole of the fittings of the sacrarium were the same as at the Coronation of George IV., and these details are from the *Gazette* description of that ceremony. Their accuracy far exceeds our aptitude at describing internal decorations. The curious in such matters will also be pleased to know that the pattern of the carpet of the theatre was in excellent taste – mullions and squares, crimson and cloth of gold colour, alternately, and a rich gold colour fringe. The cloth of gold on the steps of the throne was superb: the very surface was pure gold, over the Wilton carpet which covered the steps as well as the floor. The embroidery of the chair, or throne, was extremely rich; that of the pulpit, crimson velvet, panelled with gold, was chastely elegant, as it should be, rather than magnificent.

On the south side of the sacrarium was the box provided for the female branches of the Royal Family, and also for the young Princes. On the north side was placed a bench for the Bishops, who were to assist in the ceremonies. There were also in the sacrarium a chair of recognition and a Litany chair for each of their Majesties. St. Edward's Chair stood on the south side, and the Queen's Chair on the north of the area in front of the altar.

We have already described this chair at some length. On this occasion it was covered with gold frosted tissue, and a corresponding cushion: the crockets and fretwork were also richly gilt.

At the back of the altar, on each side, was an entry to the Traverse, or part of the Shrine of Edward the Confessor, by which their Majesties separately retired to be disrobed. These entrances were concealed by green and gold tapestry hangings corresponding with the adjoining gallery fronts.

Above the sacrarium was the gallery for the Members of the House of Commons, rising almost to the uppermost windows. This was entirely filled, two-thirds of the members appearing in various uniforms, and the remainder in court dresses. The Speaker occupied a plain oak chair in the centre, closely over the altar; before him lay his mace on a purple cushion.

At the extreme end of the Abbey, and above this gallery, in the

132

vaultings, were stationed part of the King's state band, with trumpets and drums, to aid the ceremony occasionally.

Such was the interior of the Abbey before the commencement of the ceremonies. The doors were opened at four o'clock, from which hour till ten o'clock the company continued to arrive. Lord Tenterden was first among the Peers, and so early as 5 o'clock, his lordship, (with characteristic promptitude,) was pacing the theatre, coronet in hand, and engaged in anxious inquiries. Soon after 9 o'clock all the Peers and Peeresses were present, and their separate arrivals enabled the spectators to fill up the time with notes of the splendid dresses, some of which, in our hearing, would not discredit any chronicle of fashion. The rivalry of diamonds among the peeresses was extremely superb; and the ermined robes of the peers, groves of feathers, and the richness and variety of uniforms and costumes – all observable in the transepts, made them not the least brilliant portion of the Abbey. The dulness of plain dress occasionally served to heighten the effect by contrast; but this was very partial. The choristers wore surplices and scarlet mantles, and the band half military costume. The peers did not take their seats on their entrance: their places were denoted by their names written on paper and sown on the cushioned benches, so that scores of their lordships left their coronets in their places, and betook themselves over to the peeresses, while others joined in conversational groupes nearly over the whole of the theatre. A signal gun announcing the start of the King from St. James's, however, put an end to these colloquies; a busy stir ensued, and their lordships were seated by half-past ten o'clock.

The Great Officers of State, the Archbishops of Canterbury and York, the noblemen appointed to carry the Regalia, and the Bishops who were to support their Majesties, and to carry the Bible, &c., had in the meantime arrived at the Abbey, in procession from the House of Lords.

An anthem was played by the choir, and at its close the loud and long-continued huzzas of the multitude on the outside of the Abbey announced the near approach of their Majesties. The officers of arms and the Dean and Prebendaries of Westminster, habited in their splendid stoles, marshalled themselves in the nave, along with the Great Officers of State, to receive them. At this moment the interest was intense. The Guards in the Abbey were under arms – such of the peers and peeresses as were to join the procession, moved down the aisle to take their places – the officers of the Earl Marshal were busily employed in preserving due regularity and order. Gradually, but slowly, the heralds were observed to advance. As they put themselves in motion, the glittering of the Regalia came in view. Shortly afterwards the waving plumes and gorgeous robes of the Princesses of the Blood Royal attracted general attention. The Noblemen bearing the Queen's Regalia preceded their Royal Mistress into the Abbey, and the clash of presented arms, and the enthusiastic acclaim of the spectators nearest the western door, informed those that were more distant of her Majesty's arrival. A short pause took place – then another advance – till by degrees, the line of the procession extended itself in magnificent array in the Abbey. At length His Majesty, made his appearance, and was received with applauding shouts. The choir immediately

133

commenced the anthem, 'I was glad when they said unto me we will go into the house of the Lord', and this anthem lasted until the procession had reached its destination, and their Majesties had arrived at the theatre. The procession moved in the following manner:—

FORM OF THE PROCEEDING OF THEIR MAJESTIES FROM THE WEST DOOR OF THE ABBEY INTO THE CHOIR

Officers of Arms

The Prebendaries and Dean of Westminster

His Majesty's Vice Chamberlain

Comptroller of His Majesty's Household	Treasurer of His Majesty's Household, bearing the Crimson Bag with the Medals
The Lord Chamberlain of His Majesty's Household; his Coronet carried by a Page	The Lord Steward of His Majesty's Household; his Coronet carried by a Page
The Lord Privy Seal; his Coronet carried by a Page	The Lord President of the Council; his Coronet carried by a Page

The Lord Chancellor of Ireland; attended by his Purse Bearer; his Coronet carried by a Page

The Lord High Chancellor; attended by his Purse Bearer; his Coronet carried by a Page

The Lord Archbishop of Canterbury, in his Rochet, with his Cap in his hand; attended by two Gentlemen

PRINCESSES OF THE BLOOD ROYAL, viz.:

Her Royal Highness the Duchess of Cambridge, in a Robe of Estate of Purple Velvet, wearing a Circlet of Gold on her head; her Train borne by a Lady of Her Royal Highness's Bedchamber, assisted by a Gentleman of Her Royal Highness's Household; the Coronet of Her Royal Highness borne by Viscount Villiers

Her Royal Highness the Duchess of Cumberland, in a like Robe; her Train also so borne; and the Coronet of Her Royal Highness borne by Viscount Encombe

Her Royal Highness the Duchess of Gloucester, in a like Robe of Estate; her Train borne in like manner; and the Coronet of her Royal Highness borne by Viscount Deerhurst

The Queen's Vice Chamberlain

THE QUEEN'S REGALIA, viz.:

The Ivory Rod with the Dove, borne by Earl Cawdor; his Coronet carried by a Page	The Lord Chamberlain of her Majesty's Household; his Coronet carried by a Page	The Sceptre with the Cross, borne by the Earl of Jersey; his Coronet carried by a Page
Two Sergeants at Arms	Her Majesty's Crown, borne by the Duke of Beaufort; his Grace's Coronet carried by a Page	Two Sergeants at Arms

THE QUEEN,

Five Gentlemen Pensioners	The Bishop of Winchester	in her Royal Robes; Her Majesty's Train borne by the Duchess of Gordon, in the absence of the Mistress of the Robes, assisted by Six Daughters of Earls, viz.:	The Archbishop of Armagh	Five Gentlemen Pensioners

134

Lady Teresa Fox Strangways	Lady Theodosia Brabazon
Lady Mary Pelham	Lady Georgiana Bathurst
Lady Sophia Cust	Lady Georgiana Grey

Ladies of the Bedchamber in Waiting, viz.:

Countess Brownlow	Marchioness of Westmeath

Maids of Honour, viz.:

Hon. Miss Eden	Hon. Miss De Ros	Hon. Miss Seymour
Hon. Miss Bagot	Hon. Miss C. Boyle	Hon. Miss Mitchell

Women of the Bedchamber, viz.:

Lady Caroline Wood	Lady William Russell

THE KING'S REGALIA, viz.:

St. Edward's Staff, borne by the Duke of Grafton; his Coronet carried by a Page	The Golden Spurs, borne by the Marquess of Hastings; his Coronet carried by a Page	The Sceptre with the Cross, borne by the Duke of St. Albans; his Coronet carried by a Page
The Third Sword, borne by the Marquess of Cleveland, his Coronet carried by a Page	Curtana, borne by the Marquess of Salisbury, his Coronet carried by a Page	The Second Sword, borne by the Marquess of Downshire, his Coronet carried by a Page

Black Rod   Garter

The Deputy Lord Great Chamberlain of England, his Coronet borne by a Page

PRINCES OF THE BLOOD ROYAL, viz.:

His Royal Highness the Duke of Gloucester, in his Robes of Estate, carrying his Baton as Field Marshal: his Coronet borne by a Gentleman of His Royal Highness's Household: his Train borne by Lord Edward Thynne

His Royal Highness the Duke of Sussex, in like Robes: his Coronet carried by a Gentleman of His Royal Highness's Household: his Train borne by Lord John Spencer Churchill

His Royal Highness the Duke of Cumberland, in like Robes, carrying his Baton: his Coronet borne by a Gentleman of His Royal Highness's Household: his Train borne by Lord Ernest Bruce

The High Constable of Ireland, Duke of Leinster, his Coronet borne by a Page	The High Constable of Scotland, Earl of Errol, his Coronet borne by a Page

The Earl Marshal of England, with his Staff: his Grace's Coronet borne by a Page	The Sword of State, borne by Earl Grey: his Coronet carried by a Page	The Lord High Constable of England, the Duke of Wellington, with his Staff, and his Baton as Field Marshal; his Grace's Coronet borne by a Page

A Page carrying the Staff of the Lord High Steward

The Sceptre with the Dove, borne by the Duke of Richmond; his Coronet carried by a Page	St. Edward's Crown, borne by the Lord High Steward; the Duke of Hamilton	The Orb borne by the Duke of Somerset; his Coronet carried by a Page
The Patina borne by the Bishop of Carlisle	The Bible borne by the Bishop of Chichester	The Chalice borne by the Bishop of Rochester

A Page carrying the coronet of the Lord High Steward

Ten Gentlemen Pensioners, with their Standard Bearer

Ten Gentlemen Pensioners with their Lieutenant

THE KING,

in

His Royal Crimson Robe
of State:
His Majesty's Train
borne by
Six eldest sons of Dukes,
viz.:

The
Bishop of
Bath
and
Wells

The
Archbishop
of York in
the absence
of the
Bishop of
Durham

The Marquess of Worcester   The Earl of Surrey   The Earl of Euston
The Marquess of Douro   The Marquess of Titchfield   The Earl of Lincoln
Assisted by the Master of the Robes; and followed by the Groom of the Robes
The Groom of the   The Gold Stick of the Life Guards   The Master of the
Stole; his Coronet   in waiting; his Coronet borne   Horse; his Coronet
borne by a Page   by a Page   borne by a Page
The Captain of the Yeomen of the   The Captain of the Band of Gentlemen
Guard; his Coronet borne by a Page   Pensioners; his Coronet borne by a Page
Two Lords of the Bedchamber, viz.:
Earl Amherst;   Earl of Denbigh;
Each attended by a Page to bear his Coronet
Exons of the Yeomen of the Guard   Yeomen of the Guard
Exons of the Yeomen of the Guard

As his Majesty entered the choir the procession was visible in its whole length, and was one long trail of glittering splendour, which happily beamed on those who had been stationed to view the spectacle since five o'clock. The Procession then filed off.

The Princesses and their attendants were conducted by the Officers of Arms to their box.

The Queen, preceded by her Majesty's Vice-Chamberlain, Lord Chamberlain, and the Noblemen bearing her Regalia, and attended as before mentioned, ascended the Theatre, and passed on the north side of her Throne to the Chair of State and Faldstool provided for her Majesty on the east side of the Theatre, below her Throne, and stood by the side Chair until his Majesty's arrival.

The Princes of the Blood Royal were conducted to their seats, as Peers, by the Officers of Arms.

The King, ascending the Theatre, passed on the south side of his Throne to his Chair of State, on the east side of the Theatre, opposite to the Altar; and their Majesties, after their private devotion (kneeling on their Faldstools), took their respective seats; the Bishops, their supporters, standing on each side; the Noblemen bearing the Four Swords on his Majesty's right hand; the Deputy Lord Great Chamberlain and the Lord High Constable on his left; the Great Officers of State, the Noblemen bearing his Majesty's Regalia, the Dean of Westminster, Garter, and Black Rod, standing about the King's Chair, and the Train-bearers behind his Majesty.

The Queen's Officers, the Noblemen who bore her Majesty's Regalia, her supporters, Train-bearer, and assistants, standing near her Majesty; her Lord Chamberlain on the right hand, her Vice-Chamberlain on the left; and the Ladies-Attendants behind her Majesty's Chair.

The Queen and King, as they advanced up the choir, were enthusiastically received: and all men cried 'God save them.'

136

The first of the ceremonies was

THE RECOGNITION

As soon as the anthem was concluded, the Archbishop of Canterbury, accompanied by the Lord Chancellor, the Deputy Lord Great Chamberlain, the Lord High Constable, and the Earl Marshal, preceded by Garter, advanced towards the east side of the theatre. From this position the Archbishop made the recognition in the following words:

'Sirs, – I here present unto you King William IV., the rightful inheriter of the Crown of this realm; wherefore all ye that are come this day to do your homage, service, and bounden duty, are ye willing to do the same ?'

The reply to this demand, which was delivered with great solemnity of manner, and in a clear and distinct voice, was a general and hearty acclamation of 'God save King William the Fourth.'

The recognition was repeated from the south, west, and north sides of the theatre; at each repetition the reply was still, 'God save King William the Fourth'; and at the last recognition there was a flourish of trumpets and beat of drums. The King's scholars of Westminster School, who were placed in the corner of the lower gallery, at the south side of the Abbey, and near the organ loft, immediately made a short Latin recitation, under the direction of one of their masters, which concluded with a shout of 'Vivant Rex et Regina.' The young rhetoricians were loyally vehement.

Then followed another Anthem, taken from Psalm xxi. ver. 1–6.: 'The King shall rejoice in thy strength, O Lord,' which was sung by the choir; their Majesties being in the mean time seated in their chairs of state.

We consider the Recognition as one of the most impressive stages of the whole ceremony. The King, on taking off his cap of state, was visibly affected. His Majesty bowed graciously and repeatedly to the Peers and Peeresses, and the whole scene was of that touchingly gratifying description – that mixture of sympathy and joy which can be better conceived that described.

THE OFFERING

The altar and the approaches thereto were now prepared for the solemnity of the *'Offering'*. The Bible, the Patina, and the Chalice, were placed upon the altar by the Bishops who had borne them in the royal procession.

Upon the steps of the altar the officers of the wardrobe spread a costly cloth of gold, and two splendid cushions for their Majesties to kneel on. The Archbishop of Canterbury then put on his cope, and the Bishops who were appointed to the duty of reading the Litany also vested themselves in their copes. The King, attended by two Bishops as his supporters, and preceded by the Dean of Westminster, and by the Great Officers and Noblemen, bearing the Regalia and the Four Swords, proceeded towards the altar. Here his Majesty, uncovered and kneeling, first offered a pall, or altar-covering of cloth of gold, which he placed in the hands of the Archbishop of Canterbury, who placed it on the altar. The King's second offering was an Ingot of Gold, weighing one pound, which was, in like manner delivered to the Archbishop, who put the Ingot into the oblation basin.

The Queen's offering was a pall of gold cloth, similar to that of the King, and her Majesty presented it with the same formalities as the King had presented his.

Their Majesties continuing to kneel before the Altar, the following prayer was offered up by the Archbishop of Canterbury:

'O God, who dwellest in the high or holy place, with them also who are of an humble spirit, look down mercifully upon these thy servants, William our King and Adelaide our Queen, here humbling themselves before thee at thy footstool, and graciously receive these oblations, which, in humble acknowledgement of thy sovereignty over all, and of thy great bounty to them in particular, they have now offered up unto thee, through Jesus Christ our only mediator and advocate. Amen.'

This prayer being concluded, all the Regalia, with the exception of the swords, were delivered to the Archbishop of Canterbury, who handed them to the Dean of Westminster, who placed them upon the Altar. Their Majesties were then conducted to chairs of state, covered with damask figured cloth, on the south side of the Altar. Around his Majesty's chair all the Great Officers and Noblemen who had taken part in the procession arranged themselves; the distinguished personages who bore the swords being most prominently stationed. Her majesty was surrounded by the principal officers of her household, by the Mistress of the Robes and her assistants, the Ladies of the Bedchamber, and the Maids of Honour: the latter were tastefully dressed in white muslin over satin, profusely festooned and garlanded with white roses; the chaste simplicity of these dresses excited much admiration.

The Litany was then read by the Bishop of Lichfield and Coventry and the Bishop of Lincoln, their Majesties kneeling.

The commencement of the Communion Service followed. The Bishop of Llandaff reading the Epistle, from 1 Peter, ii. 18 – 'Submit yourself to every ordinance of man, for the Lord's sake,' &c.; and the Bishop of Bristol reading the Gospel, from Matt. xxii. 15 – 'Then went the Pharisees, and took counsel how they might entangle him in his talk,' &c.

Then followed the sermon preached by the Bishop of London, his text being the passage just quoted from the Epistle of St. Peter. Their Majesties sat in their chairs opposite the pulpit. The King wore a superb cap of crimson velvet, turned up with ermine. The Archbishop of Canterbury sat in his purple velvet chair, on the north side of the altar. The Garter stood beside his Grace; The Bishops (most of whom were present,) sat on a long bench, covered with purple damask extending from the Archbishop's chair, immediately opposite to their Majesties.

The Altar was now very gorgeous, laden with service-plate of massive gold, and glittering with the splendid Regalia. The grouping, too, of the Royal Supporters, presented a scene of the most graceful and dignified character.

THE OATH

The sermon being concluded, the Archbishop of Canterbury approached the King, and standing before him addressed his Majesty thus: – Sir, are you willing to take the oath usually taken by your predecessors.' The King answered, – 'I am willing.'

The Archbishop then put the following questions to the King, whose replies were made from a book which his Majesty held in his hands.

Archbishop.—Will you solemnly promise and swear to govern the people of this kingdom of Great Britain, and the dominions thereunto belonging, according to the statutes in Parliament agreed on, and the respective laws and customs of the same?

King.—I solemnly promise so to do.

Archbishop.—Will you, to the utmost of your power, cause law and justice in mercy to be executed in all your judgments?

King.—I will.

Archbishop.—Will you, to the utmost of your power, maintain the laws of God, the true profession of the Gospel, and the Protestant Reformed Religion established by law? And will you maintain and preserve inviolate the settlement of the Church of England, and the doctrine, worship, discipline, and government thereof, as by law established within the kingdom of England and Ireland, the dominion of Wales, the town of Berwick-upon Tweed, and the territories thereunto belonging, before the union of the two kingdoms? And will you preserve unto the Bishops and Clergy of England, and to the churches there committed to their charge, all such rights and privileges as by law do or shall appertain unto them, or any of them?

King.—All this I promise to do.

His Majesty then arose out of his chair, and, attended by his supporters, went bare headed to the altar, where, kneeling upon a cushion, at the steps of the altar, and laying his hand upon the holy gospels, he said—

'The things which I have here before promised, I will perform and keep, so help me, God.'

Hereupon the King kissed the book, and signed the oath – the implements of writing being handed to his Majesty on a silver standish by the Lord Chamberlain. The King again put on his cap of crimson velvet, and returned to his chair. The anthem, 'Come, Holy Ghost, our souls inspire', was then sung by the choir.

THE ANOINTING

Upon the conclusion of this anthem, the Archbishop read the following prayer, preparatory to the anointing:—

'O Lord, Holy Father, who by anointing with oil didst of old make and consecrate Kings, Priests, and Prophets, to teach and govern thy people Israel, bless and sanctify thy chosen servant William, who by our office and ministry is now to be anointed with this oil, and consecrated King of this realm: strengthen him, O Lord, with the Holy Ghost the Comforter, confirm and stablish him with thy free and princely spirit, the spirit of wisdom and government, the spirit of council and ghostly strength, the spirit of knowledge and true godliness, and fill him, O Lord, with the spirit of thy holy fear, now and for ever. Amen.'

At the end of this prayer, the choir sang Handel's splendid Coronation Anthem, taken from I Kings, i. 39–40: 'Zadock, the priest,' &c. During the performance of this Anthem, the King was disrobed of his crimson robes; his Majesty took off his Cap of State, and the Robes and Cap were immediately carried into St. Edward's Chapel. Thus disrobed, his Majesty appeared in the uniform of an Admiral; in black trousers, with broad gold lace.

The King then proceeded to St. Edward's chair; a rich canopy, called the 'Anointing Pall', was now held over His Majesty's head by the Dukes of Leeds, Rutland, Newcastle, and Northumberland. This pall was made of gold and silver brocade; it was lined with silver tabby, and had a deep gold fringe and tassels all round it. It was raised into a canopy by the noble dukes just mentioned, by means of four silver staves, which they fixed in loops that were attached to each corner of it. The Dean of Westminster stood by St. Edward's chair, behind the Archbishop, holding the Ampulla, which contained the consecrated oil of which the Dean poured some into the anointing-spoon; into which the Archbishop dipped his fingers, and anointed His Majesty in the form of a cross, on the head, breast and hands.

We should add, that merely a drop of oil suffices. The Archbishop then pronounced a blessing.

THE INVESTING WITH THE SUPERTUNICA,

though set down in the Programme, was omitted, at the King's request. The Supertunica was, however, placed ready on the Table, but removed without being used.

THE SPURS

Immediately after the 'anointing', the Dean of Westminster took the spurs from the altar, and delivered them to the Deputy Lord Great Chamberlain; who, kneeling down, touched His Majesty's heels with them.

THE SWORD

Earl Grey, who bore the sword of state, now delivered it to the Lord Chamberlain, and in lieu thereof, received from his Grace another sword, in a scabbard of purple velvet; upon which Earl Grey delivered it to the Archbishop, who laid it on the altar, saying the following prayer:

'Hear our prayers, O Lord, we beseech Thee, and so direct and support thy Servant King William, and vouchsafe by thy right hand of Majesty, to bless and sanctify this sword, wherewith this thy servant William desireth to be girt, that it may be a defence and protection of churches, widows, and orphans, and all thy servants, and a terror to all those who lie in wait to do mischief, through Jesus Christ our Lord, Amen.'

The Archbishop, assisted by other Bishops, delivered the Sword into the King's right hand, and the Lord Great Chamberlain then girt His Majesty with it, the Archbishop saying,

'Receive this Kingly Sword, which is hallowed for the defence of the Holy Church, and delivered unto thee by the hands of the Bishops, though unworthy, yet consecrated by the authority of the Holy Apostles; and remember of whom the Psalmist did prophesy, saying, "Gird thyself with thy sword upon thy thigh, O thou Most Mighty, and with this Sword exercise thou the force of equity, and mightily destroy the growth of iniquity. Protect the Holy Church of God and his faithful people; defend and help widows and orphans; restore things gone to decay, and maintain those restored, that doing thus thou mayest be glorious in the triumphs of virtue, and excellent in the ornament of justice, and reign for ever with the Saviour of the World, whose image you bear, who with the Father and the Holy Ghost liveth and reigneth world without end." '

140

Sir George Bellew, Garter Principal King of Arms
The Duke of Norfolk, Earl Marshal

OFFERING OF THE SWORD

After this exhortation, the King rising up, went to the altar, where his Majesty offered the Sword in the scabbard (delivering it to the Archbishop), and then retired to his chair: the Sword was then redeemed by the nobleman who first received it, and who carried it during the remainder of the solemnity, having first drawn it out of the scabbard, and delivered the latter to an officer of the wardrobe.

THE INVESTING WITH THE MANTLE

His Majesty then standing in front of his chair, was invested by the Dean of Westminster with the Imperial Mantle, or Dalmatic Robe of Cloth of Gold, the Deputy Lord Great Chamberlain fastening the clasps thereof. The richness of this robe can scarcely be described. The ground, or outside, is shot with gold thread, brocaded with gold and silver, with large and small flowers of the same frosted; all the ornaments and flowers being edged about with purple, or deep Mazarine blue. Its splendour would even figure in the elaborate pages of Hall, the chronicler.

THE ORB

The King then sitting down, the Archbishop having received the Orb from the Dean, delivered it into the King's right hand, saying, 'Receive this imperial Robe and Orb; and remember that the whole world is subject to the power and empire of God,' &c. The King then returned the Orb. It has been customary at former coronations for the King to receive also the Armill, or rich arm-covering, but this was dispensed with.

THE RING

The Lord Chamberlain then delivered the Ruby Ring on a crimson cushion, to the Archbishop, who put it on the fourth finger of the King's right hand, saying, 'Receive this Ring,' &c.

THE SCEPTRES

The Archbishop then delivered the Sceptre with the Cross into his Majesty's right hand, saying, 'Receive this Royal Sceptre,' &c.: and then the Sceptre with the Dove, saying, 'Receive the Rod of Equity,' &c. The Duke of Norfolk, as Lord of the Manor of Worksop, supported his Majesty's right arm for a time, and afterwards relieved the King, by holding the Sceptre; his Grace had previously presented to the King a glove for his Majesty's right hand, embroidered with the arms of Steward, which the King put on.

THE CROWNING

This and the Recognition were the most interesting of all the Ceremonies. The Archbishop, standing before the Altar, and having St. Edward's Crown before him, took the same into his hands, and consecrated and blessed it with the prayer, 'O God, who crownest thy faithful servants with mercy,' &c. Then the Archbishop, assisted by other Bishops, came from the Altar, the Dean of Westminster carrying the Crown, and the Archbishop took and placed it on His Majesty's head, (at *one o'clock*, to a minute,) while the spectators, with loud and repeated shouts, cried, 'God save the King,' &c. the trumpets sounding, the drums beating, and the Tower and Park guns firing by signal. The acclamation ceasing, the Archbishop pronounced the Exhortation, 'Be strong and of a good

141

courage,' &c. The choir then sung the Anthem – 'The King shall rejoice in thy strength,' &c. As soon as the King was crowned, the Peers put on their Coronets, the Bishops their Caps, and the Kings of Arms their Crowns.

THE HOLY BIBLE

The Dean then took the Holy Bible from the Altar, and delivered it to the Archbishop, who, attended by the rest of the Bishops, presented it to the King, saying, 'Our Gracious King,' &c. The King then returned the Bible to the Archbishop, who gave it to the Dean, to be by him replaced on the Altar.

THE BENEDICTION

The King then knelt, holding both the Sceptres which had been already presented to him in his hands, and the Archbishop thus blessed him:—

'The Lord bless thee and keep thee; and, as he hath made thee King over his people, so may he still prosper thee in this world, and make thee partaker of his eternal felicity in the world to come.'

The Bishops then in an audible voice answered 'Amen.'

The Archbishop then turning to the people, said:—

'And the same Lord grant that the clergy and people gathered together for this ordinance, may by his gracious assistance be continually governed by thee in all happiness, and that humbly obeying his will, and faithfully serving thee, they may enjoy peace in the present life, and with thee be made partakers of the everlasting kingdom.'

Again the Bishops responded – 'Amen.'

The King then arose and went to King Edward's chair, where he kissed the Archbishop and Bishops who were present. This done, the choir sang the Hymn, *Te Deum laudamus*, or, We praise thee, O God, &c.

THE ENTHRONIZATION

When the *Te Deum* was ended, the King, led up by the Archbishops and Bishops, ascended the Theatre, and was enthroned by Bishops and Peers; and the Archbishop standing before him, pronounced the Exhortation, 'Stand firm and hold fast,' &c.

A loud and general exclamation of 'God save the King!' accompanied by clapping of hands and huzzaing now burst from every part of the Abbey. At this moment, too, the coronation medals were thrown about by the Treasurer of his Majesty's Household.

THE HOMAGE

His Majesty then delivered the Sceptre with the Cross to the Duke of Norfolk, to hold the same in his right hand, and the Sceptre with the Dove to the Duke of Richmond, to hold the same in his left hand during the homage.

The Archbishop and other Bishops then knelt before the King, and, for himself and the other Lords Spiritual, pronounced the words of the Homage, as follows:—

'I, William, Archbishop of Canterbury, will be faithful and true, and faith and truth will bear unto you, our Sovereign Lord, and your heirs, Kings of Great Britain; and I will do and truly acknowledge the service of the lands which I claim to hold of you as in right of the church. So help me God.'

These words were repeated after his Grace by the other Bishops, kneeling and paying homage in the same manner.

The Archbishop then rose and kissed his Majesty's left cheek, and touched his Crown, and after him the rest of the Bishops present did the like, and retired in their respective seniorities.

The Duke of Cumberland ascended the steps of the throne, and, taking off his coronet, kneeling before the King, pronounced for himself and the other Dukes of Blood Royal, the words of Homage, the rest doing the same with him and saying after him, *mutatis mutandis*:—

'I, Ernest Augustus, Duke of Cumberland, do become your liege man of life and limb, and of earthly worship, and faith and trust I will bear unto you, to live and die against all manner of folks – So help me, God.'

The Duke of Cumberland then kissed his Majesty's left cheek, and touched the Crown upon his head; the rest of the Dukes of the Blood Royal doing the like after him, and then retired. The Dukes and other Peers then observed the same ceremony, the senior of each degree pronouncing the words of homage. Each Peer kissed his Majesty's left cheek and touched his Crown, according to rank. To some it was an inconvenient form, inasmuch as trying to retire facewards to the King, a few aged Peers stumbled and fell. The Duke of Cumberland was nearly tripped up by the Duke of Gloucester inadvertently treading on his robe. Several Peers were much cheered as they retired: the Duke of Wellington received this meed of applause, as did Lords Plunkett and Lyndhurst. The most marked approbation was, however, shown towards Earl Grey and the Lord Chancellor. When Lord Brougham approached his Majesty, the applause was of that vehement description which bore the gale of high popular favour. The Members of the House of Commons were especially enthusiastic, and rising *en masse*, waved hats, handkerchiefs, and programmes in token of their respect.

Much time was lost to the spectators during the puerile form of kissing his Majesty, and more than once the homage appeared to him disagreeably fatiguing. The public feeling towards the Peers, however, relieved the scene; while the scramble for the medals in the choir, if not entirely decorous, was amusing. Hustle ensued upon hustle, till the King's chair appeared to be endangered by the 'robustious struggle'.

THE ANOINTING, CROWNING, AND ENTHRONING THE QUEEN
During the Coronation of the King, her Majesty the Queen had remained seated in her chair on the south side of the Altar.

As soon as the last Anthem was concluded, the Queen rose from her chair, and being supported as before, proceeded to the Altar, attended by her Train-bearer and ladies-assistants, where her Majesty knelt whilst the Archbishop said the prayer of Consecration, as follows:

'Almighty and everlasting God, the fountain of all goodness, give ear, we beseech thee, to our prayers, and multiply thy blessings upon this thy servant, whom in thy name, with all humble devotion, we consecrate our Queen. Defend her always with thy mighty hand, protect her on every side, that she may be able to overcome all her enemies; and that with Sarah and Rebecca, Leah and Rachael, and all other blessed and honourable women, she may multiply and rejoice in the fruit of her womb, to the honour of the kingdom and the good government of thy church, through Christ our Lord, who vouchsafed to be born of a Virgin that he might redeem the world, who liveth and reigneth with Thee in unity with the Holy Ghost world without end.'

This prayer concluded, her Majesty rose and went to the faldstool at which she was to be anointed and crowned, placed before the Altar between the steps and King Edward's chair; and standing there, the chief attendant took off the circlet, which her Majesty wore up to this time. This was a rim or circle of gold, richly adorned with large diamonds, and beautifully set with a string of pearls round the upper edge.

The Queen then knelt down, and four Duchesses holding a rich pall of silk, or cloth of gold, over her Majesty, as the four Dukes had held a pall over the King, the Archbishop poured the consecrated oil upon her head, saying, 'In the name of the Father, the Son, and the Holy Ghost, let the anointing of this oil increase thine honours, and the grace of God's Holy Spirit establish them for ever and ever. Amen.'

The ladies then opened her Majesty's apparel for the anointing on the breast, which the Archbishop performed, using the same words, after which he said a prayer.

One of the ladies in attendance (having first dried the place anointed with fine cotton wool) then closed the Queen's robes at her breast, and afterwards put a linen coif upon her head.

The Archbishop next put the ring on the fourth finger of her Majesty's right hand, saying, 'Receive this ring,' &c.

The Archbishop then took the Crown from the Altar, and reverently placed it on the head of the Queen, saying, 'Receive the crown of glory, honour, and joy; and God, the Crown of the Faithful, who by our episcopal hands, though most unworthy, hath this day set a crown of pure gold upon thy head, enrich you with wisdom and virtue; that after this life you may meet the everlasting Bridegroom, our Lord Jesus Christ, who, with the Father, and the Holy Ghost, liveth and reigneth for ever and ever. Amen.'

At this moment a sun-beam fell on her Majesty's Crown, which, though much less in size than the King's diadem, was of equal brilliancy. The Coronets of the Peeresses were very elegant, though they in part concealed the jewels interspersed in their hair; they were of various sizes, some so small as to appear perked on the head. The Peers' Coronets, with few exceptions, did not add much to their Lordships' dignity; the general disadvantage was in the Coronets being too large, and thus falling over the forehead. The Lord Chancellor, who wore his Coronet over his forensic wig, appeared to suffer some inconvenience by the double covering; he repeatedly evinced signs of perspiration and fatigue, by applying his handkerchief to his face. His Lordship joined ardently in the applause of the King; and, high in stature as in popular favour, the Chancellor waved his Coronet as freely as loyal heart could wish.

Her Majesty being crowned, all the Peeresses present put on their

Coronets; and then the Archbishop placed the Sceptre and the Cross in her Majesty's right hand, and the ivory Rod with the Dove in her left, and offered a short prayer. The Queen, being thus anointed and crowned, and having received all her ornaments, the choir sang the Hallelujah Chorus.

At the commencement of the chorus the Queen arose, and, supported as before, ascended the theatre (reverently bowing to his Majesty as she passed the Throne,) and was conducted to her own Throne on the left hand of that of the King, where her Majesty reposed until the conclusion of the chorus. Immediately that the chorus was over, a loud shout of 'God save the Queen' resounded through the Abbey.

THE HOLY SACRAMENT

After the chorus and homage, the two Bishops who had read the Epistle and the Gospel received from the Altar, by the hands of the Archbishop, the Patina and the Chalice, which they carried into St. Edward's Chapel, and brought from thence the bread upon the Patina, and the wine in the Chalice. Their Majesties then descended from their Thrones and went to the Altar, where the King, taking off his Crown, delivered it to the Deputy Lord Great Chamberlain to hold, and the Sceptres to the Dukes of Norfolk and Richmond. Then the Bishops delivered the Patina and Chalice into the King's hands, and his Majesty delivered them to the Archbishop, who reverently placed the same upon the altar, covering them with a fair linen cloth. The Queen also took off her Crown, and delivered it to her Lord Chamberlain to hold, and the Sceptres to those noblemen who had previously borne them.

Their Majesties then went to their chairs on the south side of the area. When the Archbishop and the Dean had first communicated, their Majesties approached the Altar and received the Sacrament, the Archbishop administering the bread, and the Dean of Westminster the cup.

The King and Queen then put on their Crowns, and took the Sceptres in their hands as before, and again repaired to their Thrones, supported and attended as when they left them.

The Archbishop then read the Communion Service, and pronounced the blessing; and at the conclusion the trumpets sounded and the drums beat.

After this, his Majesty, attended as before, the four Swords being carried before him, descended into the area, and passed through the door on the south side of the Altar into St. Edward's Chapel; and the nobleman who had carried the regalia received them from the Dean of Westminster, as they passed by the Altar into the Chapel. The Queen, at the same time descending from her Throne, went into the same Chapel, at the door on the north side of the Altar. Their Majesties then came into the Chapel, the King standing before the Altar, delivered the Sceptre with the Dove, which his Majesty had borne in his left hand, to the Archbishop, who laid it on the Altar. His Majesty was then disrobed of his Royal Robe of State, and arrayed in his Royal Robe of purple velvet by the Deputy Lord Great Chamberlain. The Archbishop then placed the Orb in his Majesty's left hand.

The noblemen who had carried the Gold Spurs and St. Edward's Staff, delivered them to the Dean, and the latter deposited them on the Altar.

Whilst their Majesties were in St. Edward's Chapel, the officers of arms arranged the return, so that all was ready to move at the moment that the King and Queen left the Chapel.

Their Majesties, and the Princes and Princesses, then proceeded out of the choir, and to the west door of the Abbey, attended as before, their Majesties wearing their Crowns; the King bearing in his right hand the Sceptre with the Cross, and in his left the Orb; and the Queen bearing in her right hand her Sceptre with the Cross, and in her left the ivory Rod with the Dove; their Royal Highnesses the Princes and Princesses wearing their Coronets, and the Princes who are Field Marshals carrying their batons. The four Swords were borne before the King in the same order as before. The Dean and Prebendaries, and the Bishops who had carried the Bible, the Chalice, and the Patina, remained in the choir. The noblemen who had severally carried the Crowns, the Orb, the Sceptre with the Dove, the Spurs, and St. Edward's Staff, walked in the same places as before; those who had staves and batons carrying the same; all Peers wearing their Coronets; and the Archbishops and the Bishops supporting their Majesties, wearing their caps; and the kings of arms their Crowns.

The whole of the Coronation Ceremonies in the Choir of the Abbey were finished by three o'clock, when the procession returned through the Choir and nave. On reaching the West door, the King's style was proclaimed by Garter King at Arms: the Regalia were returned to the robing-rooms, adjoining the new Portico, to the State officers who had borne them thither; and at about half-past three o'clock the King and Queen entered the State-carriage to return to St. James's Palace, both their Majesties wearing their crowns; a proof that they had studied the gratification of the people beyond the programme of the day.

We have purposely omitted all description of the out-door procession of their Majesties from St. James's to the Abbey. It included nearly the whole of the Royal suite, and must have been a gratifying picture of kingly splendour. Nevertheless, besides the auspicious occasion for which this pageant was arranged, the spectacle is nearly as grand on the King's visits to the House of Lords. Its importance can therefore scarcely be considered paramount with the details of the Ceremonies within the Abbey. The countless crowds assembled to view the procession on its progress to and from the Abbey, exceed our calculation, as we witnessed them through the circular windows of the vaultings, and the loopholes of the walls. This was indeed a curious *coup d'œil*, inasmuch as it showed clustering myriads on the housetops and living streams in the streets below. The joyful expressions of the multitude were distinctly heard within the choir of the Abbey, both on the approach and return of their Majesties, and combined with the pealing organ, the roar of guns, the clang of military music, and the firing of bells, – they gave rise to feelings which it were difficult to suppress.

The arrival of their Majesties at the Palace was announced by the firing of a Royal salute of 21 cannon, which closed this part of the ceremonies of the day.

Reflecting awhile upon the merited enthusiasm of the people towards our beloved Sovereign, we were forcibly reminded of the virtues which were essential to a monarch's lasting popularity, as powerfully drawn by an old dramatist:

'Tis not the bared pate, the bended knees,
Gilt tipstaves, Tyrian purple, chairs of state,
Troops of pied butterflies, that flutter still
In greatness' summer, that confirm a prince;
'Tis not th' unsavoury breath of multitudes,
Shouting and clapping with confused din,
That makes a prince. No—he's a king,
A true king, that dares do aught save wrong,
Fears nothing mortal but to be unjust;
Who is not blown up with the flattering puffs
Of spungy sycophants, who stands unmov'd,
Despite the justling of opinion;
Who can enjoy himself, maugre the throng,
That strive to press his quiet out of him;
Who sits upon Jove's footstool,
Adorning, not affecting majesty;
Whose brow is wreathed with the silver crown
Of clear content; this is a king,
And of this empire every man's possess'd
That's worth his soul.

APPENDIX B

PLAN OF THE REGALIA PROCESSION
AT THE CORONATION OF QUEEN ELIZABETH II

St Edward's Staff,
borne by the
Earl of Ancaster

The Sceptre with the Cross,
borne by the
Viscount Portal of Hungerford

A Golden Spur,
borne by the
Lord Churston

A Golden Spur,
borne by the
Lord Hastings

The Third Sword,
borne by the
Duke of Buccleuch

Curtana,
borne by the
Duke of Northumberland

The Second Sword,
borne by the
Earl of Home

Norroy and Ulster
King of Arms,
Sir Gerald Wollaston

Lyon,
King of Arms,
Sir Thomas Innes
of Learney

Clarenceux,
King of Arms,
Sir Arthur William
Steuart Cochrane

The Right Hon. the
Lord Mayor of London,
Sir Rupert de la Bere

Garter, Principal King
of Arms, Hon. Sir
George Rothe Bellew

The Gentleman Usher
of the Black Rod,
Lieut.-Gen. Sir Brian
Gwynne Horrocks

The Lord Great Chamberlain,
The Marquess of Cholmondeley

The Lord High
Steward of Ireland,
the Earl of
Shrewsbury

The Deputy to the Great
Steward of Scotland,
the Earl of Crawford and
Balcarres

The High Constable of
Scotland, Lord Kilmarnock
(deputising for the
Countess of Erroll)

The Earl Marshal, the
Duke of Norfolk

The Sword of State,
borne by the
Marquess of Salisbury

The Lord High
Constable of England,
Viscount Alanbrooke

The Sceptre
with the Dove,
borne by the Duke of
Richmond and Gordon

St Edward's Crown, borne by the
Lord High Steward,
Admiral of the Fleet the
Viscount Cunningham of Hyndhope

The Orb,
borne by the
Earl Alexander
of Tunis

The Paten, borne by
the Bishop of London,
the Right Rev. and
Right Hon. John
William Charles Wand

The Bible, borne by
the Bishop of Norwich,
the Right Rev.
Percy Mark Herbert

The Chalice, borne by
the Bishop of Win-
chester, the Right Rev.
Mervyn George Haigh

THE QUEEN

APPENDIX C

LIST OF THE REGALIA IN THE JEWEL HOUSE

I. CROWNS AND DIADEM

1. King Edward the Confessor's Crown
2. The Imperial State Crown
3. The Imperial Indian Crown
4. Crown of Queen Mary of Modena
5. Crown of Queen Mary, Consort of King George V
6. Diadem of Queen Mary of Modena
7. Crown of the Prince of Wales (as eldest son of the King)
8. Crown of Queen Elizabeth the Queen Mother
9. Queen Victoria's small Diamond Crown

II. SCEPTRES AND RODS

1. The King's Royal Sceptre
2. The King's Sceptre with the Dove, or Rod of Equity
3. The Queen's Sceptre with the Cross
4. The Queen's Ivory Rod (carried by a Queen Consort)
5. Mary II's Sceptre with the Dove
6. St. Edward's Staff

III. ORBS

1. The King's Orb
2. The Queen's Orb

IV. RINGS

1. The King's Coronation Ring
2. The Queen's Coronation Ring
3. Queen Victoria's Coronation Ring

V. SWORDS

1. The King's Jewelled State Sword
2. The Sword of State
3. The Sword Spiritual
4. The Sword Temporal
5. Curtana, or Sword of Mercy

VI. SPURS AND BRACELETS

1. St. George's Gold Spurs
2. Gold Bracelets

VII. MACES

1. Charles II
2.   Do.
3. James II
4.   Do.
5. William and Mary
6.   Do.
7.   Do.
8. George I

VIII. ECCLESIASTICAL PLATE

1. The Ampulla, or Golden Eagle
2. The Anointing Spoon
3. The Royal Baptismal Font of Charles II
4. Alms Dish of William and Mary
5. Chalice of William and Mary
6. One Chalice
7. Three Patens
8. Altar Dish
9. Flagon
10. Baron

IX. STATE TRUMPETS AND BANNERS

1. Fifteen Silver State Trumpets
2. Ten Bannerets

X. ROYAL GOLD PLATE

1. Queen Elizabeth's Salt Cellar
2. King Charles II's Salt Cellar (State Cellar)
3.   Do.
4.   Do.
5.   Do.
6.   Do.
7.   Do.
8.   Do.
9.   Do.
10.   Do.
11.   Do.
12.   Do.
13.   Do.
14. King Charles II's Wine Fountain
15. Twelve Salt Spoons
16. Two Tankards (George IV)

XI. OTHER PLATE AND VALUABLES

1. The Maundy Dish of Charles II
2. Set of Maundy Money 1d., 2d., 3d., 4d.
3. King James II's Monde
4. Model of Cullinan Diamond as found

APPENDIX D

CORONATION EVENTS

May 26.   Queen Mary's birthday.

May 27.   The Queen, with the Duke of Edinburgh, will attend a luncheon to be given by the Commonwealth Parliamentary Association in Westminster Hall.

May 28.   The Queen will give a garden party at Buckingham Palace.

May 30.   State visits of royal and official guests begin. Government evening reception.

June 1.   Morning reception by the Queen of representatives of member countries of the Commonwealth overseas. Luncheon party by the Queen for Prime Ministers and representatives of member countries of the Commonwealth overseas.

June 2.   Coronation. Commonwealth broadcast at 9 p.m. (B.S.T.) by the Queen.

June 3.   The Queen, with the Duke of Edinburgh, will drive through east London during the afternoon. The Queen will hold a state banquet at Buckingham Palace.

June 4.   The Queen, with the Duke of Edinburgh, will drive through north London during the afternoon. (Epsom meeting, Oaks.) The Queen will hold a state banquet at Buckingham Palace.

June 5.   Foreign envoys and deputations will be received by the Queen. Dinner to the Queen by the Secretary of State for Foreign Affairs. The Queen will hold an evening reception at Buckingham Palace.

June 6.   State visits of royal and official guests end. (Epsom meeting, Derby.)

June 8.   The Queen, with the Duke of Edinburgh, will drive through south London during the afternoon. The Queen, with the Duke of Edinburgh, will be present at a gala performance at the Royal Opera House, Covent Garden.

June 9.   The Queen, with the Duke of Edinburgh, will attend a service at St. Paul's Cathedral. The Queen, with the Duke of Edinburgh, will drive through west London during the afternoon. Dinner party by the Prime Minister to Commonwealth Ministers. Government evening reception.

June 10.   The Duke of Edinburgh's birthday. (Royal Tournament opens at Earls Court.)

June 11.   The Queen's birthday. Trooping the Colour on Horse Guards Parade. Fly-past by the Royal Air Force.

June 12.	The Queen, with the Duke of Edinburgh, will lunch at Guildhall. The Queen will hold an evening reception at Buckingham Palace.
June 13.	The Queen, with the Duke of Edinburgh, will visit Windsor and Eton.
June 15.	Review of the Fleet by the Queen.
June 16–19.	The Queen, with the Duke of Edinburgh, will be present at the Royal Ascot meeting.
June 20.	(Ascot Heath meeting.)
June 23–29.	The Queen, with the Duke of Edinburgh, will visit Scotland.
June 30.	The Queen will hold an investiture at Buckingham Palace.
July 2 & 3.	The Queen, with the Duke of Edinburgh, will visit Northern Ireland.
July 4.	The Queen, accompanied by the Duke of Edinburgh, will inaugurate the planting of a grove of oak trees in Windsor Park in commemoration of the Coronation.
July 5.	Review by the Queen of ex-service men and women.
July 6.	The Queen, with the Duke of Edinburgh, will be present at an evening reception to be held by the London County Council at County Hall.
July 7.	The Queen will hold an investiture at Buckingham Palace. The Queen, with the Duke of Edinburgh, will be present at a ball at Hurlingham, to be given jointly by the Royal Empire Society, the Victoria League and the Overseas League.
July 9 & 10.	The Queen, with the Duke of Edinburgh, will visit Wales.
July 14.	The Queen will hold an investiture at Buckingham Palace. The Queen, with the Duke of Edinburgh, will be present at a tattoo at the White City, to be held under the auspices of the Soldiers', Sailors' and Airmen's Families Association.
July 15.	Review of the Royal Air Force by the Queen at Odiham, Hants.
July 16.	The Queen will give a garden party at Buckingham Palace.
July 17 & 18.	(Ascot Heath meeting.)
July 21.	The Queen will hold an investiture at Buckingham Palace.
July 23.	The Queen will give a garden party at Buckingham Palace.
July 24.	The Queen will hold an investiture at Buckingham Palace.

ACKNOWLEDGEMENTS

The following illustrations are reproduced by courtesy of the persons or firms named: Plate 1, Dorothy Wilding; Plate 30, Mirrorpic; Plates 31, 32, 36, 40, A. C. K. Ware; Plate 33, Topical Press Agency; Plates 34, 35, Press Photo Combine; Plate 37, Keystone; Plate 42, Baron; Endpapers, Woman's Illustrated.